Live A Flourishing Life

By Rita Schiano

The Reed Edwards Company
Sturbridge, MA

The Reed Edwards Company

The Reed Edwards Company
P.O Box 434
Sturbridge, MA 01566

Web site: www.reededwards.com

Statements or descriptions are informational only. *Live A Flourishing Life* is not intended to be a substitute for professional medical advice for which your healthcare professional is your best source. If you believe you may need or benefit from care, you should consult a psychologist or other licensed health/mental health professional.

Purchaser shall be solely responsible for determining the adequacy of this material, and the application of this material shall not be subject to any implied warrantee of fitness for that purpose.

For information regarding permission, please write to:
Permissions Department
The Reed Edwards Company
P.O. Box 434
Sturbridge, MA 01566

Schiano, Rita.
Live a flourishing life -- 1st ed.

ISBN-13: 978-0-9795347-4-4
ISBN-10: 0-9795347-4-7

Library of Congress Catalog Number: 2010930661

Cover Art and Design by David Jarratt
Book Typography & Composition by: RMS Freelance Writing and Editorial Services
Printed in U.S.A.

Table of Contents

Part Three: Wisdom to Live By

Part Four: Relax and Flourish

Bibliography

About the Author

Acknowledgments

I'd like to express my deep appreciation for Dr. Ron Breazeale, with whom I had the pleasure of working with on the *Duct Tape Isn't Enough: Survival Skills for the 21st Century* resilience-training program. My interest in stress management and resilience began when I edited his book, *Reaching Home*, a novel about conquering fear. Over the past several years, Dr Breazeale has been a mentor, sharing his knowledge and insights, and encouraging me to work as a resilience trainer and coach. Thank you, Ron….

To learn more about Dr. Breazeale and *Duct Tape Isn't Enough: Survival Skills for the 21st Century*, as well as the Maine Resilience Project, please visit www.reachinghome.com.

Most importantly, this book is dedicated to Kim G., who urged me to develop a stress management and resilience-building course for the students in the One-Day Program at Bay Path College…to Kathy Jarret for presenting it to the powers-that-be, and to the nineteen wonderful, women students who braved the first offering of the Stress Management college course and who inspired my writing of this workbook.

Foreword

There are a number of books on stress reduction and resilience. *Live A Flourishing Life* takes a unique approach in that it blends philosophical wisdom with self-evaluating exercises to help readers discover how to live the Good Life.

The vernacular, like the author, is conversational and vibrant. The work is well-organized and easy-to-use. I like that the book is multi-purpose, whether used in a classroom, a workshop setting, or on one's own, the reader will benefit greatly from the wisdom within.

One of my favorite sections is *Kaizen!* — which focuses on the practice of implementing change by taking small steps. Rita advocates making very small changes on a daily basis, which in turn, will add up to huge results. She has given you all the tools you will need. Now, all you just have to do is use them!

I believe *Live A Flourishing Life* will be a valuable and timeless work; a book you will read, use, and re-read and re-use again and again for your entire life.

~ Dennis McCurdy, author, *Find A Way: A Guide to Getting the Most Out of Life*
and founder of the Adam Beck Institute

The Greeks Got It...
And So Can You

The notion of living the good life can be traced back to the ancient Greek philosophers — to Socrates, Plato, Aristotle, and Epicurus. These ancient thinkers revered the concept of *eudaimonia,* a classical Greek word commonly translated as happiness, well-being, or flourishing.

Now while we modern-day folk tend to think of happiness as a state of mind related to joy or pleasure, philosophers such as Epicurus thought in terms of living the Good Life — the ideal way for a person to live.

Epicurus wrote that physical pleasure and freedom from pain were significant goals for human life. Our highest pleasure — tranquility and freedom from fear — is obtained by knowledge, friendship, and living a virtuous and temperate life. "To live one's entire life in happiness," he wrote, "the greatest by far is the possession of friendship... a handful of true friends."

Epicurus regarded philosophy, first and foremost, as a form of therapy for life, since "philosophy that does not heal the soul is no better than medicine that cannot cure the body." The Good Life, thus, was a life free of mental anxiety; a life open to the enjoyment of other pleasures.

A century before Epicurus, Plato and Aristotle explained *eudaimonia* as being a byproduct of having a virtuous character. By virtue we mean a character trait or quality that is valued as being always good in and of itself. Personal virtues are characteristics valued as promoting individual and collective well-being. Therefore, a person's actions and decisions should be guided by consideration for the interests and well-being of oneself and other people.

Virtue is something that is practiced and thereby learned — it is habit (*hexis*). In the *Nichomachean Ethics,* Aristotle writes that there are two times in our lives when our character is shaped. The first is when we are children. At this time our habits and attitudes are shaped by our parents and our early teachers, who taught us the best they knew how based on what they learned. While these early rules and habit formations were central to our character development, sometimes these lessons were negative.

[1]Usener, Hermann. *Epicurea*. Leipzig: Teubner, 1887.

Our adult conception of the world, however, comes from within and is self-directed. Thus, Aristotle states, we need to look back at those early lessons, those habits we developed, and determine if they serve us or if they are habits that do not serve us. And then we must ask ourselves, "Is this the kind of person I want to be?"

Aristotle writes of living in the mean, in balance between excess and deficiency. When writing of courage, the strength of character necessary to continue in the face of our fears, Aristotle explains that courage is the mean between hubris (excess) and cowardice (deficiency).

> The man, then, who faces and who fears the right things and from the right
> motive, in the right way and from the right time, and who feels confidence
> under the corresponding conditions, is brave.

Without courage, we are unable to take the risks necessary to achieve some of the things we most value in life. To risk asking someone out on a date; to risk showing genuine vulnerability; to risk trying an academically challenging program.

To have any single strength of character in full measure, a person must have the other ones as well. Courage without good judgment is blind. It is taking risks without knowing what is worth the risk. Courage without perseverance is short-lived; and courage without a clear sense of one's own abilities is foolhardy.

To live a flourishing life is to live in the mean of self-love:
- Having feelings of care, appreciation, and respect for others
- Valuing yourself
- Knowing yourself — a long, often arduous, and never completed task
- Acting in ways that promote your genuine flourishing

The deficiency of self-love includes
- self-loathing
- too little self-valuing: self-deprecating
- too little self-knowledge — an unwilling or unable to look at one's own motivations, feelings
- too little acting — not taking steps to insure one's own well-being

The excesses of self-love take many forms, such as:
- arrogance, conceit, egoism, vanity, and narcissism
  - too much caring: self-centeredness
  - too much self-valuing: arrogance, conceit
  - too much self-knowledge: narcissistic
  - too much acting for self: selfishness

And, lastly, to live a comfortable life is to live in the mean between greed (excess) and squalor (deficiency). Living in the mean, living in balance, promotes human flourishing.

As you work through this book, the commentary, quizzes, exercises, and journaling will help you dig deep into your life story. You will uncover and discover the longstanding attitudes and habits that influence your life.

As Socrates said, "The unexamined life is not worth living." It is in examining and understanding the larger context of our lives that we can live a more flourishing life.

> *Human flourishing involves the rational use of one's individual human potentialities, including talents, abilities, and virtues in the pursuit of his freely and rationally chosen values and goals.*
> ~ Edward W. Younkins

Part One:

Managing Stress

The Process Of Change

To successfully develop and implement a stress management and resilience-building plan, one must be committed to the change process. Change is not easy; old habits die hard. Change is especially hard when a behavior or attitude is longstanding, or involves an addictive substance. (Just ask anyone attempting to quit smoking.) And change is stressful.

Change requires:
- thinking differently;
- acting differently; and
- commitment.

The Transtheoretical Model of Change

For more than a decade, James Prochaska and Carlo DiClemente of the University of Rhode Island have been studying the change process looking, initially, at how people change health habits, such as smoking. They concluded that people cycle through a five-step change process:

1. Pre-contemplation
2. Contemplation
3. Preparation and decision
4. Action
5. Maintenance

Pre-contemplation

In this first stage, the person is not thinking seriously about changing and is not interested in any kind of help. There is a tendency to defend current bad habit(s), and the person does not feel the behavior (or attitude) is a problem. The person may exhibit defensiveness — feeling change is being imposed upon him or her.

Contemplation

In the second stage there is some awareness of the personal consequences of the bad habit. At this point the person is considering the possibility of changing, although he or she is ambivalent. The person will cycle through weighing the pros and cons of quitting or modifying the behavior (or attitude), at times doubting that the long-term benefits will outweigh the short-term costs.

On the positive side, the person is more open to receiving information about the bad habit, and is more likely to reflect on his or her own feelings and thoughts concerning the habit and seek some form of intervention.

Preparation and decision

In this stage, the person is getting ready for, and has made a commitment to, making a change. He or she is no longer ambivalent.

- "I've got to do something about this — this is serious. Something has to change. What can I do?"

Action

In stage four, the person has come to believe that he or she has the ability to change the behavior, and now will be actively involved in taking the necessary steps. At this point in the process, the person needs specific information, tools, and guidance for implementing change. He or she may seek a therapist or attend a self-help group, such as Alcoholics Anonymous (AA). The key to success at this stage is to analyze and understand behavior change efforts in a way that enhances self-confidence and sustains motivation.

Maintenance

The final stage focuses on maintaining new patterns of behavior. When the response becomes automatic, the person is then able to successfully avoid any temptations to return to the bad habit. By this point in the change process program, the person has reformulated the rules of his or her life, and has acquired new skills for dealing with life and avoiding relapse. The person is now able to anticipate situations in which a relapse could occur and prepare coping strategies in advance.

Now, let's begin…

Understanding Stress and Its Effects On The Body

STRESS

- The body's reactions to a mentally or emotionally disruptive or upsetting condition; to adverse external influences capable of affecting physical health

Your body reacts to stress long before your mind becomes conscious of the stressful circumstance or condition. Many of us are so accustom to stress that we are blind to the effects that stress has on our bodies. This is why your first line of defense in stress management is your ability to identify your body's reaction to stress so that when those symptoms occur, you are mindful that stress-reducing actions must be taken.

There are a few ways to begin stress awareness. First, listen to your words, for our language often betrays us. For example, when my mother was under stress, she'd say, "My blood is boiling! My blood is boiling!" And when my brother and I would hear those words coming out of her mouth, that was our cue to hightail it out of her way…. Mom was about to blow.

But her words were an accurate reflection of her bodily response to stress. She did have the sense that her 'blood was boiling' because she had extremely high blood pressure. Even with medication, she had a tough time managing her hypertension.

So think about your language. Do you say…

- I feel like my head is in a vise
- My heart is banging in my chest
- My face is on fire
- My blood is boiling

Often, too, if we commonly refer to someone who causes us stress as a "pain in the neck" or a "pain in the a--," most often we are feeling muscle tension in our neck or lower back.

So listen to your language. And when you hear your stress words coming out of your mouth, give yourself a mental whack to the back of the head. *

* A whack to the back of the head: 1) A non-injurious head slap; 2) An old, and affectionate, Italian way of knocking some sense into us.

Along with awareness of your language, it is vital to become familiar with your body's reaction to stress. Muscle tension, such as chronic neck or back pain, is a common way our body lets us know when we are stressed.

Physical Signs the Body Is Under Stress

- Blood pressure remains up
- Heart and respiration rates stay elevated
- Sweating
- Pupils may remain dilated
- Digestion ceases

Stress Effects on the Autonomic Nervous System

The sympathetic nervous system (SNS) turns on the fight-or-flight response, a series of biochemical changes that prepare us to deal with threats or danger. Fight-or-flight is primordial, a mechanism that allowed primitive man to escape the dangers of lions and tigers and bears. When we experience excessive stress — whether from internal worry or an external circumstance — a bodily reaction occurs:

- *Fight* ---------- Charge In

- *Flight* --------- Run Away

We tend to perceive everything in our environment as a possible threat to our survival. By its very nature, the fight-or-flight system bypasses our rational mind and moves us into "attack" mode.

In contrast, the parasympathetic nervous system (PNS) promotes the relaxation response. Like sparring partners skillfully testing one another, the SNS and PNS maintain metabolic equilibrium by making adjustments whenever balance is disrupted.

The *sympathetic* and *parasympathetic* branches act together to maintain homeostasis. They are *reciprocal systems*: when one is up, the other is down. The autonomic nervous system functions involuntarily (automatically) and controls internal organs:

15

- Lungs (breathing rate)
- Heart (heart rate)
- Stomach (digestion and peristalsis — wave-like contractions of muscles that move food through GI tract)
- Blood vessels (blood pressure and temperature regulation)
- Glands (sweat and secretion of hormones)

The *sympathetic nervous system* causes the organs to prepare for action:

- **Increases**
  - breathing rate
  - blood pressure
  - heart rate
  - pupils dilate
  - sweating
  - stress hormones

- **Decreases**
  - digestion
  - saliva

The *parasympathetic nervous system* causes the organs to slow and rest:

- **Decreases**
  - breathing rate
  - heart rate
  - blood pressure
  - pupils dilate
  - sweating

- **Increases**
  - digestion
  - saliva

Hormones produced by endocrine glands serve as chemical messengers. Derived from the Greek *hormon*, "to set in motion," hormones travel through the bloodstream to accelerate or suppress metabolic functions.

Problems arise when stress hormones aren't properly metabolized. They remain active — injuring and even killing cells in the hippocampus, the area of your brain needed for memory and learning. Thus, it requires conscious effort to initiate your relaxation response and to re-establish metabolic equilibrium.

If not properly metabolized, excessive stress can lead to disorders of our autonomic nervous system, including:

- headache
- irritable bowel syndrome
- high blood pressure

Excessive stress can also lead to disorders of our hormonal and immune systems, creating susceptibility to:

- infection
- chronic fatigue
- depression
- autoimmune diseases
  — rheumatoid arthritis
  — lupus
  — allergies*

*Late-onset allergies to trees, grasses, or even indoor allergens like dust mites may be the result of stress hormone buildup.

Examples of Stress Triggers and Possible Symptoms

Stress Trigger	Symptom
Argument with spouse/partner	Pounding headache
Late for work	Jittery, racing heart
Another driver cuts you off	Tightness in stomach
Presentation at work/school	Sweating

The key to stress management is being able to recognize your body's response to emotional conditions and then to take steps to minimize or alleviate the stress triggers. A good tool is to keep a stress-awareness journal. This will help you recognize where your body stores tension. The more aware you become of your body's reaction to stress, the better you will be able to take steps to reduce the stress and metabolize the harmful buildup of stress hormones in your body.

What stress triggers and symptoms can you think of?

Stress Trigger	Symptom
_____	_____
_____	_____
_____	_____
_____	_____
_____	_____
_____	_____
_____	_____

Stress Versus Anxiety: A Brief Overview

STRESS

Stress, in and of itself, is not a bad thing; it is essentially the body's coping mechanism for dealing with circumstances that excite and enliven, or frighten and endanger us. Athletes, for example, use the effects of positive stress to excel at their sport, as do we when faced with certain situations, such as meeting deadlines at work.

Some of the positive effects of stress include:
- greater focus
- heightened alertness
- increased energy
- increased excitement, enthusiasm

Some of the negative effects of stress include:
- distracted thinking
- change in sleeping habits
- digestive problems
- loss of memory
- tense muscles
- heart palpitations
- indecisiveness
- inability to focus

ANXIETY

Anxiety has internal manifestations along with physiological:
- feelings of apprehension or dread
- feeling tense or jumpy
- anticipating the worst
- irritability
- restlessness
- watching (and waiting) for signs (and occurrences) of danger
- nightmares/bad dreams

Generalized anxiety disorder

Generalized anxiety disorder (GAD) is a pattern of frequent and excessive, exaggerated anxiety and worry about everyday life events with no obvious reasons for worry. These worries and fears are so constant, they interfere with one's ability to function and relax.

People with symptoms of generalized anxiety disorder:
- tend to always expect disaster
- worry incessantly about health, money, family, work, or school
- worry about a situation to an unrealistic or disproportionate degree
- daily life becomes a constant state of worry, fear, and dread

While a certain level of anxiety is considered normal, even beneficial, when the fear or apprehension becomes chronic, irrational, and interferes with life functions, it is time to consider professional assistance. Avoidance behavior, incessant worry, and loss of concentration and memory problems often stem from excessive anxiety.

Excessive anxiety includes physical responses, such as heart palpitations and digestive disruption, distorted thoughts and excessive worrying; and behavioral changes, such as being argumentative or withdrawing from social contact. Left unchecked, excessive anxiety may lead to an anxiety disorder.

Self-evaluation "Stress" Test

Okay…now that you've had a quick lesson on how stress affects the body, the following quiz will help you identify how well you are managing your stress. And while stress events are fluid, this questionnaire will help you gain insight into the way you respond to stress currently.

This is for your information only, so be honest with yourself!

Scale: **1** - Always; **2** - Frequently; **3** - Sometimes; **4** - Never

When there is tension or stress in my life, I…

1. _____ count to ten or practice a relaxation technique, such as focused, deep breathing.

2. _____ seek emotional support from others.

3. _____ find the information that I need to understand my situation.

4. _____ take time to breathe and relax.

5. _____ distract myself with activities I enjoy.

6. _____ enjoy active recreational activities.

7. _____ try to do the best I can, even in difficult situations.

8. _____ am able to communicate my needs.

9. _____ find reasons to laugh.

10. _____ think of ways that I can change the situation to make it better.

11. _____ seek out people who can offer me information or help me with my situation.

12. _____ try to keep the situation in perspective.

13. _____ force myself to come to grips with my problems even when I do not want to.

14. _____ allow myself to lean on others.

15. _____ turn to prayer or attending spiritual services of some kind.

16. _____ seek guidance from others who have been through similar situations.

17. _____ know how to calm myself down.

Live A Flourishing Life

Scale: **1** - Always; **2** - Frequently; **3** - Sometimes; **4** – Never

(continued) When there is tension or stress in my life, I …..

18. _____ hand my fate over to God.

19. _____ daydream about what it would be like if the problem didn't exist.

20. _____ readjust my existing goals to fit with the new situation.

21. _____ remind myself to focus on the good things in my life, instead of the bad.

22. _____ remind myself that things will eventually get better.

23. _____ outline a few strategies and choose the one that seems to be the best.

24. _____ try to look for the silver-lining in even the most difficult situations.

25. _____ would be willing to join a support group.

26. _____ try to spend more time unwinding with friends and/or loved ones.

For the next series of questions, please notice the change in the rating scale.

Scale: **1** - Never; **2** - Sometimes; **3** - Frequently; **4** - Always

When there is tension or stress in my life, I …..

27. _____ find myself so overwhelmed that I shut down completely.

28. _____ find it difficult to find someone to confide in.

29. _____ worry about the negative consequences of stressful events.

30. _____ am unpleasant to be around.

31. _____ end up blowing up at someone.

32. _____ blame everyone but myself for my problems.

33. _____ feel helpless.

34. _____ get angry with others.

35. _____ obsess about my problems.

36. _____ deny that there is a problem at all.

37. _____ give up.

38. _____ use alcohol and/or drugs more frequently.

39. _____ feel completely stuck with no way out.

Scale: **1** - Never; **2** - Sometimes; **3** - Frequently; **4** - Always

When there is tension or stress in my life, I…

40. _____ withdraw and avoid friends and family as much as possible.

41. _____ get into more arguments than usual.

42. _____ have difficulty sleeping.

43. _____ can hardly tolerate contact with others.

44. _____ am so preoccupied I can't concentrate on other important tasks.

45. _____ keep thinking that there's not much I can do to help myself.

46. _____ prefer to keep my problems to myself.

47. _____ am consumed by the stressful situation(s).

48. _____ find myself complaining about my problem.

49. _____ stay in bed because I can't deal with my problems.

50. _____ reject the help of others.

51. _____ find myself watching television for longs periods of time.

52. _____ have difficulty adjusting to new developments in my life.

53. _____ become reckless in my behavior to distract myself from my problems (i.e., heavy drug or alcohol use, risky sex, impulsive spending, gambling or physically dangerous activities).

For the next series of questions, please notice the change in the rating scale.
Scale: **1** - Always; **2** - Frequently; **3** - Sometimes; **4** - Never

Do you do the following?

54. _____ When a stressful situation occurs, I try to understand exactly what the issue is.

55. _____ If I think there is some research or other information available about a problem I have, I will seek it out.

56. _____ In light of new information, I am willing to change my opinions.

57. _____ I am able to forget about my problems and worries and just have fun.

Live A Flourishing Life

Scale: **1** - Always; **2** - Frequently; **3** - Sometimes; **4** - Never

Do you do the following?

58. _____I find a healthy outlet to express my emotions, such journaling or blogging, playing music, drawing.

59. _____When difficulties occur, I develop strategies or a plan of action to get me back on track.

60. _____When in an argument, I am willing to compromise.

61. _____When difficulties occur, I try to think about how lucky I am when compared with those who have even more difficult problems.

Know Your Stress Triggers

Each of us has situations that can make our heart race or our blood boil — deadlines, interviews, teenagers, to name a few. Knowing what causes you stress is vital and powerful information, and the beginning steps to living a healthier, stress-reduced life.

Referencing your answers on the Self-evaluation "Stress" Test, which stress trigger points were you able to identify?

My Stress Trigger Points

- _____
- _____
- _____
- _____
- _____
- _____
- _____
- _____
- _____
- _____
- _____
- _____

Kaizen!

Breaking tasks down into small, incremental steps…

Kaizen is a Japanese management concept for incremental (gradual, continuous) change (improvement); breaking tasks into small, manageable steps. Kaizen is also a way of life philosophy based on making little changes on a regular basis. Kaizen is about finding new, creative, and effective ways to improve one's life…from tackling the mundane to managing our stress, to attaining our life vision.

The Mundane

Case in point: I have sixteen oak trees in my front yard. Now, those of you with oak trees know that those mighty sentries insist on holding on to their leaves to the bitter end. In fact, it is not uncommon to see oak trees with clusters of dried, withered leaves still clinging to branches throughout the dead of winter.

Raking my front lawn (I won't even get into talking about raking the back half-acre) was a much-dreaded burden each autumn. I'd find myself waiting, waiting, and waiting for those darned leaves to fall…and then rushing to rake, blow, and haul (too many times to count) tarps filled with leaves into the woods before the early winter snow covered the ground.

One autumn day a few years ago while in complaint mode about this onerous task, my friend Dennis McCurdy* suggested I find a way to tackle this hassle. "Why not apply Kaizen principles to raking leaves?" he said. I laughed at the idea at first…but after a few moments, I realized his suggestion was brilliant.

Now, rather than waiting until mid-November when the majority of leaves are on the ground, and then breaking my back raking, blowing, and hauling for hours at a time, I spend 30 minutes each day commencing in October when the leaves begin to fall. Thirty minutes…no more; no less.

The benefits: No more sore back; no more stuffy nose from moldy leaves; no more stress wondering if I will beat the snow. And, I get out of my (home) office each afternoon for 30 minutes; I get 30 minutes of fresh air and sunshine; I get 30 minutes of exercise.

*Dennis McCurdy is a motivational speaker and author. I recommend his books, *Find A Way: A Guide To Getting The Most Out Of Life* and *52 Ways To Find A Way*. Visit his web site: http://www.find-away.com.

Kaizen In Practice – Stress

From the Self-evaluation "Stress" Test, which stress scenarios in which you scored a 4 can you plan to reduce to a 3, or a 3 down to a 2? And how can you apply Kaizen? What small, manageable steps can you take towards a healthier, more balanced lifestyle?

IMPORTANT: List the stress indicators below, but take Kaizen action on only one indicator at a time. Once you move that indicator from 4 to 3; 3 to 2, only then move on to the next indicator on your list.

Stress indicator from the Self-evaluation "Stress" Test

_____

_____

Kaizen action

_____

_____

Stress indicator from the Self-evaluation "Stress" Test

_____

_____

Kaizen action

_____

_____

Stress indicator from the Self-evaluation "Stress" Test

_____

_____

Kaizen action

_____

_____

_____

Stress indicator from the Self-evaluation "Stress" Test

_____

_____

Kaizen action

_____

_____

_____

Stress indicator from the Self-evaluation "Stress" Test

_____

_____

Kaizen action

_____

_____

_____

Breaking It Down

As I mentioned earlier in the text, Aristotle proclaimed that there are two times in our lives when our character is shaped. The first is when we are children. At this time our habits and attitudes were shaped by our parents and our early teachers who taught us the best they knew how based on what they learned. These early attitude and habit formations were central to our character development; and sometimes those lessons were negative.

For Aristotle, a habit or *hexis* is a determinate power to act in a specific way. Habits can foster the good life by cultivating virtue and by developing the passions to feel pleasure and pain in right ways. Happiness is the "chief good" of human life and the most basic requirement of such a life is "activity of the soul in accordance with complete excellence." (Book I, *Nichomachean Ethics*)

The next series of chapters will help you identify habits that serve you, and habits that do not. To live a flourishing life you begin by uncovering habits that affect how you think and act. Many habits operate without your conscious awareness. Changing habits begins with recognition, followed by mindful awareness and intention to adjust your thoughts and behaviors until they become habits that serve you.

To adapt habits that make you flourish, you must learn how to manage and maintain balance in your life. You need to look at your past experiences and examine how you were able to successfully change some of your patterns of behavior or attitudes.

> *Excellence is an art won by training and habituation. We do not act rightly because we have virtue or excellence, but we rather have those because we have acted rightly. We are what we repeatedly do. Excellence, then, is not an act, but a habit.*
> ~ Aristotle

Changing habitual behavior is a process. Be patient and be compassionate with yourself. Each of us creates our own journey of releasing bad habits and adopting good habits through conscious choice. Embrace those choices; embrace the changes. They are the catalysts that will improve your life.

It's Not Your Life...
It's His (or Hers)

Make somebody happy today. Mind your own business.
~ Ann Landers

Sometimes we just can't help ourselves.... We witness an event, hear a news story about something someone said or did, and we think to ourselves (or more likely say to others), "I would *never* have done that!" or "That's not how *I* would have responded."

So, ask yourself...honestly...

- Do you find yourself frustrated, annoyed, or angered by the actions (or words) of others that have nothing to do with you?
- Do you take as a personal affront situations that have nothing to do with you?
- Do you sometimes meddle in what does not concern you?

The frustration or anger that can well inside us from situations that are not only out of our control, but have nothing to do with us, chips away at our peace of mind and releases stress hormones which, left unattended, can lead to health-related problems.

Let's see how involved you are in other people's matters. True or false...

1. When I find myself eavesdropping on others' conversations, I draw conclusions. T   F

2. When I'm out to dinner, other diners' misbehaving children irritate me.   T   F

3. While my spouse (partner, friend) is on the phone, I make comments in response
   to his or her conversation.   T   F

4. People who drive cautiously drive me nuts.   T   F

Detail a scenario/situation that did not concern you, but did frustrate, anger, or annoy you.

_____

_____

_____

_____

_____

_____

_____

_____

_____

_____

_____

_____

_____

_____

_____

_____

_____

How did the above scenario/situation make you feel?

_____

_____

_____

_____

_____

_____

_____

_____

_____

_____

_____

_____

_____

_____

_____

Why do you think the scenario/situation affected you when it did not concern you?

_____

_____

_____

_____

_____

_____

_____

_____

_____

_____

_____

_____

_____

_____

_____

_____

_____

Did the scenario/situation remind you of a personal event from your past? If so, what happened and how did you respond to it at the time?

_____

_____

_____

_____

_____

_____

_____

_____

_____

_____

_____

_____

_____

_____

_____

Effective Communication and Conflict

Conflict is a critical event in the course of a relationship. Conflict can cause resentment, hostility, and perhaps the ending of that relationship. However, conflict can be productive and lead to deeper understanding, mutual respect, and closeness.

Do you shy away from conflict? Which of the following statements may reflect your approach to conflict?

- My underlying anger may get out of control.
- To me, conflict is an all-or-nothing situation.
- I find it difficult to face conflict because I feel inadequate.
- I have difficulty positively asserting my views and feelings.

There are different styles when it comes to facing conflict. For example, one person may avoid or deny the existence of conflict. With this approach, the conflict often lingers in the background during interaction creating the potential for further tension and even more conflict.

Another person may get mad and blame the other, mistakenly equating conflict with anger. This approach often serves to increase the degree of friction by amplifying defensiveness.

And then there are those persons who use power and influence to win at the other's expense. This approach to conflict allows competitive impulses to emerge. The conflict is rarely truly resolved, since the "loser" will continue to harbor resentment.

Lastly, there are those who appear to compromise but are, in fact, subtly manipulating the other person in the process. This approach perpetuates the conflict and compromises the trust.

> *Criticism is something we can avoid easily —*
> *by saying nothing, doing nothing, and being nothing.*
> ~ Aristotle

How to Reduce Conflict

The key to conflict resolution is effective communication. There are a few methods that work well.

The Defusing Technique

The goal of the diffusing technique is to address the other's anger by simply agreeing. This is accomplished by finding some truth in the other point of view, thereby making it difficult for the other person to maintain his or her anger.

- Example: I know that I said I would call you last night. You are absolutely right. I wish I could be more responsible sometimes.

Now, the accusation might be completely unreasonable from your viewpoint. However, there is always some truth in what the other person says. The point of this technique is that we need to acknowledge that people have different ways of seeing things. By seeking some truth in their message, you validate the other's point of view. This allows you to move on to a healthier resolution.

- Lesson: Respect another's point of view; ultimately, yours will be respected too.

Empathy: Putting Yourself In the Other Person's Shoes

Empathy is an important listening technique; it gives the other feedback that he or she is being heard. There are two forms of empathy:

1. **Thought Empathy**: gives the message that you understand what the other is trying to say. Paraphrase the words of the other person.

   - Example: "What you seem to be saying is..."

2. **Feeling Empathy**: acknowledging how the other person probably feels.

   - Lesson: Never attribute emotions that may not exist for the other person. Instead, indicate your perception of how the person must be feeling.
   - Example: "I think you probably feel angry or upset with me right now."

36

Exploration

Ask gentle, probing questions about what the other is thinking and feeling. Encourage the other to talk about what is on his or her mind.

- Example: "Are there any other thoughts that you need to share with me?"

Use "I" Statements

Take responsibility for your own thoughts rather than attributing motives to the other person.

- Example: "I feel pretty upset that this thing has come between us."

Stroking

Find positive things to say about the other person. Show a respectful attitude.

Let Go Of Yesterday

If you can tell a story about how you were wronged last month, last year, or five, even ten years ago with the same vehemence, anger, and ire, then *YOU HAVE NOT LET GO OF IT!*

What happened, has happened. What was done, is done, over, *finis…. LET GO OF IT* and *MOVE ON.*

What one hurt, injustice, irritation, or inconsideration are you holding on to? Write the situation below.

What happened, as you recall it:_____

_____

_____

_____

_____

_____

_____

_____

_____

_____

_____

_____

When did this happened:_____

_____

_____

Who was involved:_____

_____

_____

What was your initial reaction:_____

_____

_____

_____

_____

_____

What did you say or do at that time:_____

_____

_____

_____

_____

_____

Live A Flourishing Life

What was the outcome, at that time:_____

_____

_____

_____

_____

_____

In retrospect, would you have done or said anything differently: _____

_____

_____

_____

_____

_____

How is your relationship with the person(s) at the present time: _____

_____

_____

_____

_____

What changes/actions are you willing to take and/or make now to truly let go of this old hurt:

_____

_____

_____

_____

_____

_____

_____

Additional insights:_____

_____

_____

_____

_____

_____

The Apology

Returning again to those ancient Greeks, Plato in his writing entitled, *The Apology Of Socrates,* offers his version of the speech given by Socrates whereby Socrates defends himself against charges of being a man "who corrupted the young, refused to worship the gods, and created new deities."

This earlier meaning of 'apology,' from the Greek *απολογία,* referred to speaking in defense of a cause or of one's beliefs or actions. In modern times, apology has come to mean acknowledging one's mistake and asking for forgiveness.

Whether in reference to small oversights or major hurts, sincere apologies make it possible for relationships to continue.

Randy Pausch* in his book, *The Last Lecture,* has a chapter in which he writes a "bad apology is worse than no apology." He explains that when we hurt each other – intentionally or unintentionally — it is "like an infection" in our relationship.

Offering no apology would be like letting the infection continue, yet giving a Real Apology is like using an antibiotic salve. A bad apology is worse, Pausch writes, because "it is like rubbing salt in the wound."

Pausch provides these examples of bad apologies: (*The Last Lecture*, by Randy Pausch, 2008, pp. 161-162).

- *I'm sorry you feel hurt by what I have done.*

This statement, he explains, indicates that you really aren't interested in putting medicine on the wound. The statement has no personal acknowledgement that one's words (or actions) were hurtful. It says, in other words, "You are too sensitive. Get over it."

- *I apologize for what I did, but you also need to apologize to me for what you've done.*

In the above statement you are, in actuality, wanting an apology, not truly asking for one.

A proper apology, Pausch writes, has three steps:

1. What I did was wrong.
2. I feel badly that I hurt you.
3. How do I make you feel better?

Pausch made me think of the halfhearted attempts I have made, where I have not been as sincere as I should have been with my apologies. Even more disconcerting is the thought that I may have offended someone without knowing it, for I know at times I can be brusque.

To be responsible and accountable for one's words and actions, to apologize well, and to remember to do so when warranted, is vital to maintaining strong, sincere, and healthy relationships.

Is there someone to whom you owe an apology?

_____

_____

What was the situation, circumstance that caused the rift? How serious do you think it was?

_____

_____

_____

_____

_____

How serious did the other person interpret the circumstance to be?

_____

_____

_____

_____

How strained is the relationship because of the mistake?

_____

_____

_____

_____

_____

What are you willing to do to right the relationship?

_____

_____

_____

_____

_____

_____

* Randy Pausch was a professor of computer science and human-computer interaction and design at Carnegie Mellon University in Pittsburgh, Pennsylvania. In September 2006, Pausch learned that he had terminal pancreatic cancer. He gave an upbeat lecture entitled, _The Last Lecture: Really Achieving Your Childhood Dreams_ on September 18, 2007 at Carnegie Mellon. Pausch later co-authored a book called _The Last Lecture_ on the same theme, which became a _New York Times_ bestseller. Randy Pausch died of complications from pancreatic cancer on July 25, 2008. He was forty-eight years old.

To view a video of _The Last Lecture: Really Achieving Your Childhood Dreams_, go to: http://www.youtube.com/watch?v=ji5_MqicxSo

The Multi-tasking Miasma

It is not surprising that modern day life is often referred to as the "culture of distraction." We are bombarded with information 24 hours a day, 7 days a week. And yet, most of us cannot get enough. We channel surf, search the Web, talk and text, drive and text, drive and talk, drive and talk and text. It is no wonder we are driven to distraction!

> The term "multi-tasking" originated in the computer engineering industry and refers to the simultaneous execution of more than one program or task by a single computer processor.

Now, the human brain really is quite amazing. According to a study conducted at the University of California, San Diego, the average American consumes 34 gigabytes worth of information a day, that's about 100,000 words. Now, clearly we don't parse a full 100,000 words each day, but that rather staggering figure does infiltrate our eyes and ears and minds via the Internet, television, radio, iPods, text messaging, cell phones, video games, Wii, and oh, so much more.

Not only are we less focused, we are not present-moment oriented. And in our efforts to skim through volumes of information, we truly miss out on quite a bit by paying only partial attention.

How often do you do more than one thing at once? Take the test to find out.

Scale: **1** - Always; **2** - Frequently; **3** - Sometimes; **4** - Never

1. _____ I keep the television on in the background when I am not actively watching it.

2. _____ I have my cell phone on at all times.

3. _____ When I'm on the telephone, I often surf the Internet.

4. _____ When I'm watching television, I channel surf during commercials.

5. _____ When I'm out to lunch or dinner with others, I take non-emergency phone calls.

6. _____ I do a crossword puzzle, Sudoku, or other activity while watching television or listening to music.

7. _____ I have to have the television on at night in order to fall asleep.

8. _____ I read the newspaper or other material while at stoplights or when sitting in traffic.

9. _____ I text message when I'm in the company of others.

10. _____ When I'm on the Internet, I frequently have 3 or more browser windows open.

Which of the above would you commit to changing in order to be more present-moment oriented?

1. _____

2. _____

3. _____

4. _____

5. _____

What steps will you take to make those changes?

1._____

_____

_____

_____

_____

2._____

_____

_____

_____

_____

_____

3._____

_____

_____

_____

_____

_____

4._____

_____

_____

_____

_____

5._____

_____

_____

_____

_____

Silence...

"Silence is the great teacher,
and to learn its lessons you must pay attention to it.
There is no substitute for the creative inspiration, knowledge, and stability
that come from knowing how to contact your core of inner silence."
~ Deepak Chopra

Silence is a means of achieving mindful awareness and inner peace. Practicing silence is a way of becoming more attentive to the world around us.

On March 31, 2009, Anne D. LeClaire was my guest on my show, *Talk To Me... Conversations With Creative, Unconventional People* on Blog Talk Radio. Anne has written eight novels, including the critically acclaimed *Entering Normal, The Lavender Hour, Every Mother's Son, Sideshow,* and *Leaving Eden.* Her latest book, *Listening Below The Noise* — part memoir, part philosophical reflection — is a look at the importance of silence as a means of achieving awareness and inner peace.

> Noise is a prime environmental cause of stress. Noise pollution triggers the body's stress response releasing stress hormones into your autonomic nervous system. Studies on the effects of environmental noise show an association between noise exposure and cardiovascular disease.

Since 1992, Anne has practiced silence on the first and third Monday of each month. For twenty-four hours, she does not speak. Her commitment to silence did not come without challenges. However, she stated, the benefits derived outweigh any bumps along the road to peace and serenity.

I asked Anne what possessed her to commit to the practice of silence? Her response, in a word, ...gratitude. Gratitude called her to silence.

On that day in 1992, Anne was walking the beach near her home on Cape Cod. "It was an absolutely beautiful day... but that day I was sad because my best friend's mother was dying and I could do nothing to prevent the pain that was coming to my friend. I think that the element of a tender and sore heart was critical in what followed. I had paused to watch two eider ducks dive in the water. As they stayed underwater for an amazing length of time, I thought, 'Isn't that like a little miracle of nature that these creatures could stay submerged for longer than I could hold my breath.'" As Anne focused on the eiders, her sadness waned.

"When we start to feel gratitude* about something, it can be like a domino line." She began to think about the many things she was grateful for. "I thought, 'I am so blessed in this moment, I don't know what to do.' And at that instance, I heard someone behind me say, 'Sit in silence.'" Anne turned around; no one was there. Nothing like that had ever happened to her before or since, but the experience was so profound it called her to attention. "What could that mean? And I thought maybe it just means: Be quiet," Anne explained.

She went home and told her husband, "I'm not going to talk tomorrow." She spent the next day in silence. The experience, she said, was so profound in so many ways. It was life changing. She heard things in herself that normally were drowned out by too much chatter.

"I felt so restored and rested at the end of the day…. It slowed things down. We live in such a hectic, noisy world. For this one day I had stepped back from this crazed, media-driven, fear-based crazy world, and had just been in this moment of silence. It was so incredible. I knew I wanted to do it again."

Anne began to see what happens when we make space for creative thoughts to rise up. She began to read about sounds and how artists and musicians talk about the need for silence in the creative process. Silence, she said, has been "one of my greatest teachers, giving me a center from which to live, strengthening me, testing me, and facilitating deep healing."

The full interview with Anne D. LeClaire can be heard via the Internet on Blog Talk Radio: http://www.blogtalkradio.com/rita/2009/04/01/talk-to-meconversations-with-creative-unconventional-people-with-host-rita-schiano

Discover the Still, Small Voice Within

During a traditional Quaker meeting, the Friends sit in silent meditation. No one speaks unless they are moved to do so through the "still, small voice" of God within. As a result, spoken words are often sparse, clear, and wise.

When practicing silence, listen for that still, small voice within. How will you recognize it?

- It moves us toward love – for ourselves and others
- There is a sense of clarity, excitement, relief, an undeniable knowing

When we make life decisions by listening to the noise – and not the silence – our decisions often are colored by fear. In listening to the voice that speaks to us from within the silence, we may find all the guidance we need to take the right action.

*For more on practicing gratitude, go to p. 133.

LeClaire, Anne D. *Listening Below the Noise: A Meditation On the Practice of Silence*. New York: HarperCollins, 2009.

Introducing Silence Into Your Life

There are numerous ways to introduce silence and stillness into your life. You can make a commitment to one or two days a month, as Anne LeClaire did, or you can try one or several of the suggestions below. Use the following pages to journal your process and progress.

- When you are home alone, get out of the habit of turning on the television, radio, or sound system.

- When in the car alone, turn off your cell phone and the radio.

- If you have little ones at home, get them involved in the practice of silence. Make it a game. "Who can not speak for 5, 10, or 15 minutes?" You'll get a little break from the constant chattering of the kids, and they'll learn a valuable practice at an early age.

- Eat a meal in silence. Silent eating helps you pay closer attention to your food, enhancing the sensory experience of flavors and textures.

- Designate a certain hour or half-hour of the day as silent time, perhaps in the early morning or before bedtime.

- Go to sleep in silence.

- Take a walk in the woods or at a nature sanctuary — someplace far from the madding crowd.

- When in line at the grocery store, avoid reading the gossip rags, or joining in "complaint conversation" with others in the checkout line.

- **Which method(s) of silence did you try?**

_____

_____

_____

_____

_____

_____

_____

_____

_____

_____

_____

_____

_____

_____

_____

_____

_____

How did your time of silence make you feel?

_____

_____

_____

_____

_____

_____

_____

_____

_____

_____

_____

_____

_____

_____

_____

_____

Did you encounter resistance from within and/or from others?

_____

_____

_____

_____

_____

_____

_____

_____

_____

_____

_____

_____

_____

_____

_____

_____

How did you feel physically and emotionally?

_____

_____

_____

_____

_____

_____

_____

_____

_____

_____

_____

_____

_____

_____

_____

_____

Did you hear the still, small voice within? What did you hear?

Ten Simple Steps For Reducing Stress

1. The rush to get out of the house: Do you often run late in the morning? Are you always fighting the clock trying to get out of the house and get to work, to an appointment, or to school on time?

Here are a few time management tips:

- Get up 15 minutes earlier.
- Prepare for the morning the night before:
    — decide what you will wear to work or school the next day
    — iron your clothing
    — set up the coffeemaker
    — set the table for breakfast

What other activities can you do beforehand to alleviate the 'morning rush'?

- _____
- _____
- _____
- _____
- _____
- _____
- _____
- _____
- _____
- _____
- _____

2. Apologize for a mistake. Reducing stress involves removing the sources of stress. And sometimes, that source of stress is our own behavior. We may be curt or brusque with another person, unthinking in our actions or words.

We all make mistakes, but it is how we deal with those errors in judgment and take steps to rectify the situation that show our true character.

To whom do you feel you owe an apology?

- _____

- _____

- _____

What first step will you take to make peace?

_____

_____

_____

_____

_____

_____

_____

_____

_____

_____

_____

3. Practice gratitude. Who do you want to thank?

- _____

- _____

- _____

- _____

- _____

4. Learn to say no.

5. Laugh at something you did.

- _____

- _____

6. Keep a journal of thoughts and feelings.

7. Go for a walk.

8. Count your blessings. What are three blessings in your life?

- _____

- _____

- _____

Why are the above blessings? _____

_____

_____

_____

_____

9. Make a list…and follow it. Remember: prioritize and keep it doable. Don't set yourself up to fail!

10. Read something funny every day.

Suggested humor writers…
- Erma Bombeck
- David Sedaris
- Lily Tomlin
- Jane Wagner
- Bill Cosby
- Fannie Flagg
- Nora Ephron

Bonus tip! **Read something inspiring every day.**

> For fast acting relief,
> Try *slowing down.*
> ~ Lily Tomlin

Developing Your Stress Management Plan

The following statements can serve as a guide in developing your stress management plan. Answer the statements as thoroughly and honestly as possible. Remember: this is your guide to developing a stress management plan that will work for you.

Reducing stress is important to me because_____

_____

_____

_____

_____

_____

A significant source of stress in my life is_____

_____

_____

_____

_____

_____

_____

Reducing stress and taking better care of myself will help me in the following ways:

_____

_____

_____

_____

_____

_____

_____

_____

_____

_____

_____

_____

_____

_____

Three things I can do this week to help reduce my stress level are:

1. _____

2. _____

3. _____

Of these things listed above, the one I will try and will stick with is:

_____

_____

_____

_____

_____

The following activities/situations would help me feel better:

1. _____

2. _____

3. _____

4. _____

5. _____

6. _____

7. _____

8. _____

9. _____

10. _____

Five ways I could take better care of myself are:

1. _____

2. _____

3. _____

4. _____

5. _____

My commitment to developing and following this stress management plan will help me in the following ways:

1. _____

2. _____

3. _____

4. _____

5. _____

6. _____

7. _____

8. _____

Part Two:

Building Resilience

Self-evaluation Resilience Test

Before we delve into resilience building, the following quiz will help you identify how resilient you are currently. Again, this is for your information only, so be honest with yourself!

Scale: **1** - Always; **2** - Frequently; **3** - Sometimes; **4** – Never

1. _____ I am usually optimistic.

2. _____ I am flexible in my thinking and my actions.

3. _____ When there is a problem, I can usually find a solution.

4. _____ I am self-confident and believe in my abilities.

5. _____ In a crisis or chaotic situation, I am usually calm and focused on taking useful actions.

6. _____ I can readjust my existing goals to fit new situations.

7. _____ I see difficulties as temporary and expect to overcome them.

8. _____ I attempt to do the best I can, even in difficult situations.

9. _____ I am able to communicate my needs.

10. _____ Even during crises, I find reasons to laugh.

11. _____ I can think of ways to change a situation to make it better.

12. _____ I seek out people who can offer me information or help me with my situation.

13. _____ I try to keep discordant situations in perspective.

14. _____ I can communicate my needs.

15. _____ I am a good listener.

16. _____ I keep in close and frequent communication with my friends.

17. _____ I approach difficult situations with commonsense.

18. _____ I am usually tapped to be a group leader.

19. _____ I am non-judgmental of others.

20. _____ I believe difficult situations make me stronger.

What Is Resilience?

There are some things you learn best in calm,
and some in storm.
~ Will Cather

Resilience, as defined by the American Psychological Association, is the process of adapting well in the face of adversity, trauma, tragedy, threats, or even significant sources of stress. It is the ability to 'bounce back' to homeostasis after a disruption in our lives.

Examples of these significant sources of stress may be:
- Losing one's job
- Serious illness — oneself or a loved one
- Natural disasters
    - floods
    - paralyzing snow and/or ice storms
    - hurricanes
    - tornadoes
- Caretaking an aging, ailing parent or loved one
- Attacks on our nation

Resilience is not a trait that people either have or do not have. Rather, resilience involves behaviors, thoughts, and actions that can be learned and developed in anyone. Research on resilience has also shown us that people who cannot deal with their emotions, fear in particularly, may become more narrow-minded and rigid in their view of the themselves and their place in the world.

Building a resilience plan may reduce the frequency and intensity of post-traumatic stress disorders and other health problems that occur after a national or a personal disaster, allowing those affected to recover more quickly and completely.

As Dr. Ron Breazeale stated in his workshop, *Duct Tape isn't Enough: Survival Skills for the 21st Century,* "This 'circle-the-wagon' mentality can increase the level of paranoia in a society and result in the rejection and persecution of those who are different from the mainstream by their religion, race, sexual preference, or physical or mental ability." Witness our society's reaction to these groups during the years since 9-11.

Think back to September 11, 2001. Recall and write below how you felt in the hours, days, and weeks following those horrific events.

Were you or anyone you know a victim of the attacks?

_____

_____

_____

_____

What was your immediate reaction?

_____

_____

_____

_____

_____

_____

Did you immediately reach out to family members?

_____

_____

_____

_____

_____

If you were at work, on vacation, or out and about town, did you have the urgency to get home immediately?

_____

_____

_____

_____

_____

Did you find yourself glued to the news channels throughout that day, and the days that followed? How did you feel watching the news?

_____

_____

_____

_____

How safe did you feel?

_____

_____

_____

_____

_____

Did you participate in any religious or community memorial services?

_____

_____

_____

_____

_____

Did you have trouble sleeping?

_____

_____

_____

_____

Did you drink more alcohol, smoke more, or start smoking cigarettes since the attacks?

_____

_____

_____

_____

_____

Other personal insights

_____

_____

_____

_____

_____

_____

_____

> *Resilience is not a trait that people either have or do not have. Resilience involves behaviors, thoughts, and actions that can be learned and developed in anyone.*
> ~ The National Institute of Mental Health

It Begins With Attitude

"You are what you think, not what you think you are."
~ Bruce MacLelland

Resilience starts with attitude. Attitude about…
- One's self
- One's abilities
- One's goals and dreams

This begins with self-confidence. Self-confidence is a fundamental conviction about one's competence and abilities. Having a positive self-image is critical if a person is to have the ability to confront and manage fear and anxiety in his or her life.

A resilient attitude is about one's self-worth. Believing one is worthy of success and happiness is necessary in order to improve one's life. Our self-worth drives our motivation to succeed.

Self-confidence + Self-worth = Self-esteem

Self-esteem is the combination of our self-confidence and our self-worth. It is the unconditional appreciation of one's self. Nathaniel Branden, author of *The Power Of Self-Esteem*, wrote:

> Self-esteem is the experience that we are appropriate to life and to the requirements of life. More specifically, self-esteem is…

> 1. Confidence in our ability to think and to cope with the basic challenges of life.
> 2. Confidence in our right to be happy, the feeling of being worthy, deserving, entitled to assert our needs and wants and to enjoy the fruits of our efforts.

*We can either watch life from the sidelines, or actively participate…
Either we let self-doubt and feelings of inadequacy prevent us
from realizing our potential, or embrace the fact that when we turn
our attention away from ourselves, our potential is limitless.*
~ Christopher Reeve

Factors That Make For Resilience

Man has never made any material as resilient as the human spirit.
~ Bern Williams

1. A positive/optimistic view of yourself and confidence in your strengths and abilities.

2. The capacity to manage strong feeling, emotions, and impulses.

3. Strong communication and problem-solving skills.

4. The capacity to make realistic plans and to take steps to carry them out.

Optimism

An empowering, constructive attitude that creates conditions
for success by focusing and acting on possibilities and opportunities.
~ Max More

Factor #1: A positive/optimistic view of yourself and confidence in your strengths and abilities.

First, let me be clear. When I talk of optimism I do not mean that rose-colored glasses, Pollyannaish way of looking at the world. Optimists see tragedy just fine. Optimists know bad things happen. But what separates optimists from their pessimistic brothers and sisters is how they move forward in their thinking and actions relative to those events.

Much of the way we view the world has been shaped by the messages we received as children. (Habits that serve us; habits that don't serve us. – Aristotle) So, let me ask: Do you view yourself as an optimist or a pessimist?

I was fortunate to grow up with women who were remarkable optimists. My mother and my maternal grandmother — women who lived through great difficulties, such as the Great Depressions, single-parenting, loss of children and spouses — still managed to demonstrate the belief that things will always work out in the end.

I was well into my teenage years when I learned that not everyone grew up learning this positive outlook. A dear, childhood friend was taught differently. She received messages such as:
- Feeling good about yourself? Be forewarned. There will always be someone who can't wait to knock you down.
- Just because you did well today doesn't mean you will tomorrow.
- If you expect the worst, you'll never be disappointed.

The nice part about being a pessimist
is that you are constantly being either proven right
or pleasantly surprised.
~ George F. Will

According to Dr. Martin Seligman's theory of learned optimism, optimistic children grow up to be optimistic teenagers and adults. In his book, *Learned Optimism,* Seligman states that there are three factors that determine a learned optimistic paradigm:

1. **Optimism is acquired from our mothers.** How our mothers reacted to problems set the stage for our own reaction to difficult situations. If mom dealt with everyday problems with a bright and hopeful outlook, then we, as children, learned to do the same.
2. **Optimism is influenced by the adults around us.** The way adults (parents, teachers) chastise us can leave a lasting impression on how we perceive our own abilities. (Thank God for my mom and grandmother. I attended Catholic school in the 1960s.… Enough said.)
3. **Optimism is shaped by family turmoil.** Family crises such as divorce or the untimely or tragic death of a family member, can contribute to a child's general view of life later life.

> *A pessimist is one who makes difficulties of his opportunities;*
> *an optimist is one who makes opportunities of his difficulties.*
> ~ Harry Truman

The optimist …

- Views life positively

- Takes life as it is

- Is open to possibilities

- Has a sense of humor
    - particularly about one's self

- Is rational
    - Uses reason rather than being led by fears and desires
    - Objectively assesses situations
    - Takes action based on those assessments

> *The realist sees reality as concrete.*
> *The optimist sees reality as clay.*
> ~ Robert Brault

Reacting Versus Responding

We may not be able to control the circumstances that come our way.
We can control how we respond to them.

Factor #2: The capacity to manage strong feeling, emotions, and impulses.

As we learned in the section on managing stress, situations happen in life that are out of our control. And, like we discussed in developing your stress management plan, learning to respond to them, rather than to react, is key.

The capacity to manage strong feeling, emotions, and impulses involves being able to:

- take action without being impulsive and responding out of emotion
- put emotions to the side when clear thinking and action are required
- use thinking as a way of managing one's emotions

When we allow ourselves to get worked up, particularly over the 'small stuff,' we are needlessly causing our bodies to go into fight-or-flight mode.

Which of the statements below most accurately reflect your reacting versus responding approach?

1. When someone is talking in the movie theatre, I…
_____ sit there and seethe.
_____ inform the manager.
_____ change my seat.

2. When at a restaurant, if a party seated after me gets their food before me, I …
_____ complain to the waitress.
_____ remain patient, assuming my meal requires more preparation time.
_____ vow to never come back to this restaurant again.

3. If someone makes an illegal turn in front of me, I…
_____ yell at them and honk my horn.
_____ assume they are just an idiot.
_____ assume the person didn't realize it was an illegal turn.

4. When someone has more than 12 items in the express line, I…

_____ don't let it bother me.

_____ clear my throat and count aloud *my* 12 items and comment "just at the allowed limit."

_____ get irritated and mumble under my breath how inconsiderate some people are.

5. When in the library and people are talking, I…

_____ turn around and shush them.

_____ stand up, gather my belongings, and stomp off.

_____ turn to the people and kindly ask them to lower their voices.

Detail a scenario/situation that did not concern you but did frustrate, anger, or annoy you.

_____

_____

_____

_____

_____

How did the above scenario/situation make you feel?

_____

_____

_____

_____

_____

What action, if any, did you take?

_____

_____

_____

_____

_____

Were you able to let the frustration go quickly, or did it fester throughout the day?

_____

_____

_____

_____

What steps can you take to not let a similar situation affect you in the future?

_____

_____

_____

_____

_____

More of Life's Little Annoyances...
(Don't let them get to you)

Life's smallest annoyances disturb us the most.
~ Michel de Montaigne

Here are a few more of life's little annoyances that seem to get our blood boiling at times. By developing strong resilience skills we, in turn, develop a keen awareness of our tendency to let the little stuff get to us. Learn to let the small stuff go. Learn to view some of these situations as humorous, rather than rancorous. You just might live longer, and live a happier life.

- In a crowded parking lot someone has parked using two spaces.
- The person behind you in the supermarket runs his cart into the back of your ankle.
- There's a car riding close to your bumper when you're on the highway.
- People who don't use the turn signal.
- The person who makes that sucking sound with the straw when the glass is nearly empty.
- The dog in the neighborhood that barks at everything
- You can never put anything back in a box the way it came.
- The elevator stops on every floor and nobody gets on.
- The person who pushes the elevator button after you already did.
- You cut your tongue licking an envelope.
- The cable goes out during your favorite program.
- People who dangle their feet out the car window.
- People who put their feet on your dashboard.
- The one or two ice cubes that won't pop out of the tray.
- You forgot to check your pockets for Kleenex before you put the pants in the wash.
- The person in the car behind you who honks the horn because you let a pedestrian use the crosswalk.
- You set the alarm on your digital clock for 6:00 p.m. rather than 6:00 a.m.
- The radio station doesn't tell you the names of the songs they play.
- People behind you in line dash ahead of you to the checkout line just opening up.
- You had the keys in your hand only a second ago and now you can't find them.
- You set up the coffeemaker, then forgot to turn it on.
- When the last person to use the bathroom leaves an empty roll on the holder.

79

Strong Communication: Being Assertive

Effective communication is 20% what you know
and 80% how you feel about what you know.
~ Jim Rohn

Factor #3: Strong communication and problem-solving skills.

How you interact with people can be a major source of stress. Good communication is essential to resilience; it breeds positive emotions instead of negative ones. Assertive communication is a skill worth learning. It enables you to communicate more effectively and to minimize the number of stressful situations that will come your way in life.

Consider the following example: You and your spouse or partner had plans to go out to dinner. He or she is usually home by 6:00 p.m. Six o'clock comes and goes, as does seven, eight, and nine o'clock. You try calling his or her office. No answer. You try calling the cell phone and it goes directly to the messaging system. You cycle between worry, fear, and anger.

At 10:07 p.m., the front door opens and in walks your loved one. "So-and-so from the office is retiring so we all went out for drinks," you're told.

"We were supposed to go out to dinner tonight. I've been worried sick."

"Sorry," is the only response you get as he or she heads upstairs to the bedroom.

You feel mistreated by this lack of communication which seems to indicate thoughtlessness and a lack of caring. Instead of yelling at your significant other (an aggressive response), or simply not commenting on the lateness (a passive response), you might try talking about how you have been affected.

"I feel apprehensive when you are late because I care about you and worry that something might have happened. I would really appreciate it if you would try to let me know when you are going to be late."

This assertive statement is likely to be much more effective than saying aggressively, "You inconsiderate jerk! I'm so mad I could just scream!"

Assertive response strategies

1. **Stop!** Stop your initial angry reaction so that you can think of a more useful response.

2. **The 7-Second Rule.** Take a deep breath (or two or three, whatever you may need). Whether you take 7 seconds, 7 minutes, 7 hours, or 7 days, take whatever time is necessary to respond logically and fairly. Once you are calm, try to identify what specifically has triggered your anger so that you can defuse it. Anger distorts, rather than clarifies, a proper response.

3. **Communicate effectively**. Respond rather than react to the person who has angered you. Respond calmly. If possible and appropriate, talk about your feelings — how you were affected, as opposed to making accusations. Talking about your own experience is unlikely to make the other person defensive, and is more likely to get your message heard and understood.

Say What You Mean

There's an adage: Say what you mean, and mean what you say. (And, some might add, don't be mean when you say it.)

Philosophically, we could look to linguistic relativism, the thesis that the grammatical structures of different languages imply different conceptions of reality. And some of you smarty-pants might want to challenge this idea, noting that linguistic relativism is an empirical thesis substantiated through anthropological examples.

Sorry. Not going there….

The point is simply this: Never leave someone having to guess what you mean versus what you said.

√ Remember: communication is the key to any relationship. You can disagree without being disagreeable.

And now a message from Dr. Seuss:

> *Say what you mean and act how you feel,*
> *because those who matter don't mind,*
> *and those who do mind don't matter.*
> ~ Dr. Seuss

Strong Communication: Problem-solving

*The problems that exist in the world today cannot be solved
by the level of thinking that created them.*
~ Albert Einstein

Resilience is requisite to good leadership. The resilient leader excels in his or her ability to communicate well and problem solve. Resilient leaders are innovative. They choose effective strategies for dealing with conflicting priorities. They stay committed to change and allow themselves to be open to new ways of doing things. They inspire and mentor others.

Whether you are a resilient leader in the workplace, in the classroom, or in the home, the following aspects apply.

The Resilient Leader

- Understands commitment…
  - knows what must be done and why
  - develops action plans
  - follows action plan

- Internalization…
  - has determined possible obstacles
  - has a plan to deal with the obstacles
  - has checkpoints

- Is Responsible….
  - doesn't externalize
    — does not blame others, or their past
  - knows it is up to them
  - knows the only things they can control are their activity and behavior
  - knows it is okay to fail
  - doesn't play psychological games, such as…
    — "If it weren't for you…"
    — "Yes, but…"
  - performs the behavior needed at the appropriate times
  - learns from inappropriate behavior
  - accepts challenges
  - does not rationalize

83

- Self-Confident…
  - high self-esteem
  - is not affected by what others think
  - doesn't take a "no" as failure
  - learns from one's actions

- Controls emotions

- Is not lost for words

- Doesn't take things personally

- Knows what to say or do at the appropriate time

- Doesn't panic

- Doesn't become excitable

- Doesn't strategize "on the fly"

- Stays in the moment

- Doesn't over analyze

- Deals with problems candidly

- Displays sincerity, believability, warmth, and trust

- Is accountable…
  - to the goal
  - to overcoming weaknesses
  - to not accepting mediocrity

- Has a strong desire for success

Are You A Resilient Leader?

Using a scale of 1 (Strongly Disagree) to 5 (Strongly Agree), how do you assess your resilient leadership skills and attitudes?

1. _____ When working on group projects, I am inclined to let my ideas be known.

2. _____ I enjoy helping others to resolve interpersonal conflicts.

3. _____ Team accomplishment is more important to me than my own accomplishments.

4. _____ I like to compliment people that I work with when progress is made.

5. _____ I am energized when people count on me for ideas.

6. _____ People often take my ideas and run with them.

7. _____ When involved in group projects, building team cohesiveness is important to me.

8. _____ I have a reputation for breaking new ground.

9. _____ People rely on me for advice.

10. _____ I am methodical about collecting facts before I make a decision.

11. _____ I am an excellent listener, able to see the situation from another's point of view.

12. _____ I am firm and fair-minded when dealing with others.

13. _____ I take calculated risks and I develop contingency plans for major decisions.

How Good A Listener Are You?

Listening is an essential part of effective communication. Listening is different from hearing. Listening enhances your capacity for understanding and empathy. When you listen to what another is saying, you begin to see the world through his or her viewpoint.

How are you in a conversation? Do you get impatient? Daydream? Multi-task? Focus solely on the person talking with you? Take the test to find out.

Scale: **1** - Always; **2** - Frequently; **3** - Sometimes; **4** - Never

_____ Do you interrupt others or finish their sentences?

_____ Do you find yourself thinking, "Hurry up! Finish the story already!"

_____ When I'm on the telephone, I often engage in another activity.

_____ Do you interrupt to express your point of view?

_____ Do you ever set the phone down, or pull it away from your ear?

_____ Do you urge others to hurry up, with words like "Yeah, yeah" so you can have your turn to speak?

_____ Do you form opinions before he/she has finished talking?

_____ Do you get uncomfortable when there are pauses in a conversation?

_____ Do you often use a speakerphone when the call is solely between you and another?

_____ Are you thinking about your response while the other person is still talking?

Which of the above would you like to change?

- _____
- _____
- _____
- _____
- _____
- _____

What steps will you take to make those changes?

_____

_____

_____

_____

_____

_____

_____

_____

_____

_____

_____

Setting Goals

If you want to live a happy life, tie it to a goal, not to people or things.
~ Albert Einstein

Factor #4: The capacity to make realistic plans and to take steps to carry them out.

The 4th factor is two-pronged: it involves goal setting and time management. Goal setting helps you achieve what you want in life and, more importantly, helps reduce stress caused by procrastination, lack of preparation, and other internal battles unknown to your conscious mind.

Goals keep us on track; goals give us focus; goals give us hope.

The 5 characteristics of a goal:

1. Clear
2. Specific
3. Realistic/attainable
4. Measurable
5. Compelling

If a man knows not what harbor he seeks,
any wind is the right wind.
~ Seneca

In 1981, George Doran created the clever acronym SMART* goals as a way of changing vague vision and goal statements into reasonable, doable plans of action.

*Doran, George T. "There's a S.M.A.R.T. way to write managements' goals and objectives." *Management Review,* Nov. 1981, Volume 70 Issue 11

SMART GOALS

- **S**pecific
- **M**easurable
- **A**ttainable
- **R**ealistic
- **T**ime specific

Specific

- What, exactly, are you going to do?

Measurable

- How will you know when you've reached the goal?
- How will others know?

Attainable

- Are you capable of reaching the goal?
- Do you have the ability?
- Do you have the resources?
- Do you have the time?

Realistic

- Are you willing to commit the time, resources, or education* to reaching the goal?

Time specific

- When, exactly, are you going to start?
- What are your timelines?
- When should the goal be reached?

*Education can be anything from reading trade magazines, blogs, and books to taking formal classes.

List at least three SMART goals you will commit to attaining.

1. _____

_____

_____

_____

2. _____

_____

_____

_____

3. _____

_____

_____

_____

4. _____

_____

_____

_____

5. _____

_____

_____

_____

It's About Time ...

Don't say you don't have enough time.
You have exactly the same number of hours per day
that were given to Helen Keller, Pasteur, Michelangelo, Mother Teresa,
Leonardo DaVinci, Thomas Jefferson, and Albert Einstein.
~ H. Jackson Brown, Jr.

Time management, in a nutshell, is how we get things done. When you develop good time management skills you are in control of your time, your life, and your stress level. So, if you feel the need to be more organized, more productive, start by considering the following:

Identify Your Time Bandits

Do you set out to check your e-mail, or your Facebook page updates, or your favorite Internet news site, and suddenly find that ninety minutes has flown by? Do you set out to play fifteen minutes of online games such as Farmville, Word Twist, Rummikub "just to clear my mind" and suddenly three hours has passed you by? Meet your Time Bandits — those insidious time-wasters that steal time we could be using much more productively.

What are your Time Bandits?

_____

_____

_____

_____

_____

Establish routines and stick to them as much as possible.

While unexpected interruptions or crises will arise, you will be more productive if you have a plan of action to follow.

Set time limits for tasks.

Reading and answering e-mail can consume a large portion of your day if you are not mindful. Set a time limit of one hour a day for this task and stick to it. If checking e-mail is part of your work routine, plan no more than 4 to 6, ten-minute intervals each day.

The List

Every Sunday evening, spend 5-10 minutes writing a plan for the next week, listing the tasks you have to do. Now, many of you may be thinking, "My list has fifty tasks on it…and it seems to grow exponentially." You are not alone. We all have dozens of items that could go on our "To Do" list. The key is learning to set priorities.

Begin by detailing only one week's worth of priorities at a time. A proven technique is simply to rate your priorities: 1, 2, and 3. Mark the tasks on your list with a #1 if they are critical for your goals and absolutely must be done that day. Next, list the top three priorities. Then detail how you will go about getting the tasks done. Each time you complete a task, *cross it off the list.* The visual reinforcement of seeing items with a strikethrough mark has a positive effect on the psyche.

Number 2 tasks are less urgent, yet they do carry some importance. These are the next set of tasks that you will move up the list. Number 3 tasks are "would be great to do" tasks that you could do if you have any time left after completing #1 and #2 tasks. Number 3 tasks are those that can be safely moved to the next week, generally becoming #1s and #2s.

√ **When making a "To Do" list, remember Kaizen — break down your complex tasks into smaller manageable pieces, and focus on one at a time.**

> *Lost time is never found again.*
> ~ Benjamin Franklin

This Week's "To Do" List

Top Three Priorities

1. _____

2. _____

3. _____

Notes on how to accomplish the above: _____

_____

_____

_____

Three More Things I'd Like To Get Done

4. _____

5. _____

6. _____

Notes on how to accomplish the above: _____

_____

_____

_____

Things To Be Done, If Time Allows

- _____
- _____
- _____
- _____
- _____
- _____
- _____
- _____
- _____
- _____
- _____
- _____
- _____
- _____
- _____

√ **Move any undone items to Top Three Priorities list next week.**

√ **Move any undone items to Three More Things list next week.**

Kaizen In Practice — Tasks

What tasks do you have that overwhelm you and/or your time? And how can you apply Kaizen? What small, manageable steps can you take to manage the task?

Task

_____

_____

_____

_____

Kaizen action

_____

_____

_____

Task

_____

_____

_____

_____

Kaizen action

_____

_____

_____

Task

_____

_____

_____

_____

Kaizen action

_____

_____

_____

_____

Task

_____

_____

_____

_____

Kaizen action

_____

_____

_____

_____

Factors That Make For Resilience – Self-assessment

Which of the following factors reflect your resilient skills and attitudes?

I have the capacity to make realistic plans and to take steps to carry out those plans.

Situation:_____

_____

_____

_____

_____

_____

_____

Skills/attitudes tapped:_____

_____

_____

_____

_____

_____

97

I have a positive/optimistic view of myself, and confidence in my strengths and abilities.

Situation:_____

_____

_____

_____

_____

_____

_____

Skills/attitudes tapped:_____

_____

_____

_____

_____

_____

_____

I use my communication and problem-solving skills.

Situation:_____

_____

_____

_____

_____

_____

_____

Skills/attitudes tapped: _____

_____

_____

_____

_____

_____

_____

_____

How I rate my capacity to manage strong feeling, emotions, and impulses.

Situation:_____

_____

_____

_____

_____

_____

_____

Skills/attitudes tapped: _____

_____

_____

_____

_____

_____

_____

_____

Characteristics Of Resilient People

It is the very nature of life to strive to continue in being.
Since this continuance can be secured only by constant renewals,
life is a self-renewing process.
~ John Dewey

- **Ability to bounce back**

- **Adopt a "Where there's a will, there's a way" attitude**

- **See problems as opportunities**

- **Ability to hang tough during difficult times**

- **Have a healthy social support network**

- **Have deep-rooted faith in a system of meaning (religious or philosophical)**

- **Embrace an optimistic attitude**

The ability to bounce back

How quickly we bounce back from crises and tragedy is dependent on how resilient we are. Sometimes, however, our lack of understanding about our life experiences — or habits that don't serve us — keeps us from adapting when new stresses affect us. As we reflect upon and come to terms with our personal history, and take steps to adjust the undermining attitudes and habits, the greater will be our ability to bounce back quickly.

Adopt a "Where there's a will, there's a way" attitude

Resilient people have a penchant for learning. They have the ability to reflect upon and recognize objectively their strengths and weaknesses. This self-reflection helps them gain insight into their current circumstances, opening them to new ideas and new tactics for dealing with crises.

Resilient people have the ability to look at critical situations in a new way, finding creative approaches towards solving a problem. They recognize that life is a series of good times and not so good times, and that you need the bad to appreciate the good. Hard times build character, creating positive lessons that better equip us to cope in the future.

Ability to hang tough during difficult times

Resilient people are good at managing their emotions. They stay calm under pressure and persevere.

Have a healthy social support network

Good friends help us get through the tough times. They help us to get tasks done (clean up after a flood, for example); they listen and validate our feelings. It is important to remember that no one person can be expected to be the 'be all and end all' of support. Often it takes several friends, each of whom provide different types of support. Resilient people are good at making friends and keeping them.

Often we find that 'life' gets in the way — family obligations, kids ballgames or concerts, household tasks, to name a few — and we let those friendships slide. We have good intentions to get together, share a meal, but we keep delaying and delaying. (As the old maxim goes: The road to hell is paved with good intentions.)

If keeping in touch with those special friends has diminished to a quick e-mail, text messaging, or 140 characters on Twitter or Facebook.... *Stop!* Instead of booting up the computer, pick up the telephone. Hear the sound of your friend's voice. Meet for a 30-minute cup of coffee if a two-hour dinner date doesn't fit into your hectic schedule. Make a face-to-face connection...at least once a month, every month.

Have deep-rooted faith in a system of meaning (religious or philosophical)

In 1902, William James wrote *The Varieties of Religious Experience* in which he detailed the universal belief systems of human beings. Now, a little more than a century later, scientists report they have located the part of the brain that controls religious faith — known euphemistically as the 'God spot.' The researchers' findings support the idea that the brain's evolvement to belief systems was a means of improving our chances of survival, thus a belief in God became widespread in human evolutionary history.

Regardless as to whether God exists or not, we do know that people with religious or spiritual beliefs tend to be more content and are better able to cope with tragedies and crises. Faith acts as a stimulus, driving us to aspire to achieve the seemingly impossible. Faith drives away fear. Faith frees us from the need to be in control during uncontrollable circumstances.

> *Faith is taking the first step even when you don't see the whole staircase."*
> ~ Martin Luther King, Jr.

Embrace an optimistic attitude

Attitude really is everything. Resilient people have a sense of hope and trust in the world. They believe in the basic goodness and decency of people, trusting that things will turn out all right in the end. This positive attitude allows them to weather the bad times and gives them the ability to hope for a better future.

For more on Optimism refer to pages 74-75.

Characteristics Of Resilient People — Self-assessment

Your ability to adapt to stressful situations, personal tragedies, or crises is often determined by the strength of your resilient characteristics. The following represent characteristics of resilient people. Which of the following reflect your resiliency?

- **Ability to bounce back**

Situation:_____

_____

_____

_____

_____

_____

Which skills/attitudes helped you to bounce back from the above situation?

_____

_____

_____

_____

_____

- **Adopt a "Where there's a will, there's a way" attitude**

Situation:_____

_____

_____

_____

_____

Which skills/attitudes did you tap into?

_____

_____

_____

_____

_____

_____

_____

_____

- **See problems as opportunities**

Situation:_____

_____

_____

_____

_____

_____

How did you adjust your thinking to address the situation?

_____

_____

_____

_____

_____

_____

_____

_____

_____

- **Ability to hang tough during difficult times**

Situation:_____

_____

_____

_____

_____

_____

Which skills/attitudes did you tap into?

_____

_____

_____

_____

_____

_____

_____

_____

_____

- **Have a healthy social support network**

Situation:_____

_____

_____

_____

_____

_____

To whom did you turn for assistance and/or guidance?

_____

_____

_____

What assistance/guidance was given to you?

_____

_____

_____

_____

_____

- **Have deep-rooted faith in a system of meaning (religious or philosophical)**

Situation:_____

_____

_____

_____

_____

_____

How does your faith, spiritual, and/or philosophical beliefs/outlook guide you?

_____

_____

_____

_____

_____

_____

_____

_____

_____

• **Embrace an optimistic attitude**

Situation:_____

_____

_____

_____

_____

_____

How did embracing an optimistic attitude help you?

_____

_____

_____

_____

What, if any, negative thinking did you have to overcome?

_____

_____

_____

_____

Learning From The Past*

Most of us have gone through at least one event in our life that has challenged us to the core. The following pages will help you to examine those events and to identify the resilience skills and attitudes that you tapped; ones that you may not consciously realize or recognize that you have. Furthermore, this exercise will serve as a blueprint for any future crisis or tragedy that may come your way.

What are events (natural disaster, death of loved one, divorce, financial challenges) that I have experienced in my life that were extremely stressful to me?

_____

_____

_____

_____

_____

_____

_____

_____

_____

_____

* From _Duct Tape Isn't Enough: Survival Skills For The 21st Century_ by Dr. Ron Breazeale. © 2009
Reprinted with permission.

How have I managed these events? How did I deal with my feelings? Did I avoid talking about it? Did I think about other people I know and recall how they had dealt with similar crisis?

_____

_____

_____

_____

_____

_____

_____

_____

_____

_____

_____

_____

_____

_____

_____

_____

_____

Did I ask others for help, or did I go it alone?

Who have been my role models or mentors?

_____

_____

_____

_____

_____

_____

_____

_____

_____

_____

_____

_____

_____

_____

_____

Have I helped others through bad times? How?

_____

_____

_____

_____

_____

_____

_____

_____

_____

_____

_____

_____

_____

_____

_____

_____

Do I tend to throw myself into work or other activities as a way of coping with hard times? Is this helpful?

_____

_____

_____

_____

_____

_____

_____

_____

_____

_____

_____

_____

_____

_____

_____

What have I learned about myself, and from others, about managing difficult situations?

_____

_____

_____

_____

_____

_____

_____

_____

_____

_____

_____

_____

_____

_____

During hard times, was I able to use my head? Did I think clearly?

_____

_____

_____

_____

_____

_____

_____

_____

_____

_____

_____

_____

_____

_____

_____

_____

How did the adverse events in my life change my thinking about myself and the world in which I live?

_____

_____

_____

_____

_____

_____

_____

_____

_____

_____

_____

_____

_____

_____

Am I a stronger person for having gone through a life crisis? How so, or why do you think not?

_____

_____

_____

_____

_____

_____

_____

_____

_____

_____

_____

_____

_____

_____

_____

_____

Developing Your Resilience-Building Plan

The following statements can serve as a guide in developing your resilience-building plan. Answer the statements as thoroughly and honestly as possible. Remember: this is your guide to developing a resilience-building plan that will work for you.

How can I strengthen and build my connection to others, particularly the people in my support network?

_____

_____

_____

_____

_____

_____

_____

_____

_____

_____

_____

_____

_____

How should I change my thinking? How can I become more optimistic? How can I see things in my life as temporary, both the good and the bad, rather than permanent; as having a specific effect on certain areas of my life rather than a pervasive one?

_____

_____

_____

_____

_____

_____

_____

_____

_____

_____

_____

_____

_____

_____

_____

_____

How can I improve my planning and decision-making skills? Do I need to work on being more decisive? If so, how will I go about doing that?

How am I taking care of myself each day? Am I paying attention to the foods I eat? Am I getting some exercise each day?

_____

_____

_____

_____

_____

_____

_____

_____

How am I managing my time? Am I getting things done today rather than putting them off until tomorrow?

_____

_____

_____

_____

_____

_____

What can I do to feel more self-confident and value my self-worth?

_____

_____

_____

_____

_____

_____

_____

_____

How can I practice flexibility in my thinking and actions on a daily basis?

_____

_____

_____

_____

_____

_____

_____

What are my goals for the future?

_____

_____

_____

_____

_____

_____

_____

_____

_____

_____

_____

_____

_____

_____

_____

_____

_____

_____

My commitment to developing and following this resilience-building plan will help me in the following ways:

1. _____

2. _____

3. _____

4. _____

5. _____

6. _____

7. _____

8. _____

9. _____

10. _____

11. _____

12. _____

Live A Flourishing Life

Part Three:

Wisdom
To
Live By

Life Is What You Do...

Life is what you do
while you're waiting to die.
Life is how the time goes by
~ Zorba (Lyrics by Fred Ebb)

In 1969, Joseph Stein together with John Kander (music) and Fred Ebb (lyrics) adapted the novel *Zorba the Greek* by Nikos Kazantzakis into a Broadway musical. The show opens (and ends) with the song "Life Is," with lyrics that bolster Alexis Zorba's credo that you must grab life while you can.

In 1978-79, I was a graduate student and teaching assistant with the Philosophy Department at Miami University. One interdisciplinary course that I taught was on confronting death. During class one day I asked my students, "If you were given the option to know when you were going to die, would you want to know?"

While some said no, others were adamant about their yes. Pressing on a bit, (the following, by the way, is the Socratic method in action) I then asked, "What would be the benefit of that knowledge?"

Many students thought it would help them to plan their lives. I recall comments such as:

"If I knew I was going to die at 43, then I would work harder so I could retire sooner."

"If I'm going to die when I'm 32, then I'm not going to waste time working. I'm just gonna live."

"If I have fifty more years, then I've got plenty of time to do things."

"Interesting," I remarked. "So, if I understand you all correctly, knowing when you're going to die enables you to put off doing, to a much later date, something you would ordinarily do in the near future."

One young woman reinforced my analysis. "For example, my boyfriend and I want to get married and have kids after I graduate. But if I'm going to live to be 75, then I can put off having kids until I'm in my 30s. This way we can have ten years together, just the two of us, before we start a family."

"Is having a family important to you?" I asked.

"Absolutely! I love kids. We both do. Children would complete our marriage."

"Okay," I said. "So, knowing you would not die until you were 75 years old gives you the confidence to put off having children, which is something that is vitally important to you and your boyfriend, until you're, say, 36 years old, right?"

"Yes. I'd have the time to wait."

"Okay," I paused for dramatic effect. "What if at age 75 you died as result of injuries sustained in an accident…an accident you were in when you were 25 years old, and you had spent those 50 years in a vegetative state. What does that do to your plans?"

The class erupted.

"I never said you could know the conditions or situation that led up to or caused your death. My question was: 'If you were given the option to know when you were going to die, would you want to know?'

"The message is this," I continued. "We should not postpone things that we know we want to do. None of us will live forever; none of us know when we will die, or the state of our health throughout our lifetime. Therefore, we should try to live each day as if it were our last, and each day we should try to do one thing that brings us joy."

Forty years after the premiere of *Zorba* and nearly three decades after I blew my students' minds, screenwriter Justin Zackham wrote *The Bucket List*. The film, directed by Rob Reiner and starring Jack Nicholson and Morgan Freeman, follows two terminally ill men on their road trip with a wish list of things to do before they "kick the bucket." Some of the desires on their Bucket List included:

- Witness something truly majestic
- Help a complete stranger for the good
- Laugh till I cry
- Kiss the most beautiful girl in the world
- Get a tattoo
- Go skydiving
- Sit on the Great Egyptian Pyramids

What would you like to do, but think you do not have the time for doing so? It can be something as simple as learning the lyrics to a song you really like, or as daring as climbing Mount Rainier. Or it may be telling someone you love him or her, or that you are sorry for something you've done or said. Get started on your Bucket List. Add to it often. Make a promise to yourself to try doing one of the desires on your list each day or week.

I've allocated 60 slots. Don't let that number hinder you!

131

*A man's reach
should exceed his grasp.*
~ Robert Browning

My Bucket List

1. _____

2. _____

3. _____

4. _____

5. _____

6. _____

7. _____

8. _____

9. _____

10. _____

11. _____

12. _____

13. _____

14. _____

15. _____

16. _____

17. _____

18. _____

19. _____

20. _____

More Items On My Bucket List

1. _____

2. _____

3. _____

4. _____

5. _____

6. _____

7. _____

8. _____

9. _____

10. _____

11. _____

12. _____

13. _____

14. _____

15. _____

16. _____

17. _____

18. _____

19. _____

20. _____

More Items On My Bucket List

1. _____

2. _____

3. _____

4. _____

5. _____

6. _____

7. _____

8. _____

9. _____

10. _____

11. _____

12. _____

13. _____

14. _____

15. _____

16. _____

17. _____

18. _____

19. _____

20. _____

The Daily Decalogue of Pope John XXIII

Born Angelo Giuseppe Roncalli, Pope John XXIII was elected Pope in 1958. Known as "The Good Pope," his love for the church and for people made him one of the best-loved popes of modern times.

Realizing that the Roman Catholic Church needed renewal and reform, John XXIII brought a fresh approach to the church, which he called "opening the windows," or *aggiornmento* — a spirit of change and open-mindedness. In that spirit, on October 11, 1962 he convened the Second Vatican Council, for which he is greatly remembered.

His pontificate lasted less than five years. Yet in that short amount of time, John XXIII presented himself to the world as "an authentic image of the Good Shepherd. Meek and gentle, enterprising and courageous, simple and active, he carried out the Christian duties of the corporal and spiritual works of mercy...." (From *L'Osservatore Romano,* Weekly Edition in English, September 6, 2000.)

As part of his personal devotional life, John XXII developed a daily Decalogue — ten resolutions that he sought to observe "only for today." While his resolutions may seem daunting, the "one day at a time" approach does make them attainable.

1. Only for today, I will seek to live the livelong day positively without wishing to solve the problems of my life all at once.

2. Only for today, I will take the greatest care of my appearance: I will dress modestly; I will not raise my voice; I will be courteous in my behavior; I will not criticize anyone; I will not claim to improve or to discipline anyone except myself.

3. Only for today, I will be happy in the certainty that I was created to be happy, not only in the other world, but also in this one.

4. Only for today, I will adapt to circumstances, without requiring all circumstances to be adapted to my own wishes.

5. Only for today, I will devote 10 minutes of my time to some good reading, remembering that just as food is necessary to the life of the body, so good reading is necessary to the life of the soul.

6. Only for today, I will do one good deed and not tell anyone about it.

7. Only for today, I will do at least one thing I do not like doing; and if my feelings are hurt, I will make sure that no one notices.

8. Only for today, I will make a plan for myself: I may not follow it to the letter, but I will make it. And I will be on guard against two evils: hastiness and indecision.

9. Only for today, I will firmly believe, despite appearances, that the good Providence of God cares for me as no one else who exists in this world.

10. Only for today, I will have no fears. In particular, I will not be afraid to enjoy what is beautiful and to believe in goodness. Indeed, for 12 hours I can certainly do what might cause me consternation were I to believe I had to do it all my life.

To conclude: here is an all-embracing resolution: "I want to be kind, today and always, to everyone."

Practice Gratitude

He is a wise man who does not grieve for the things which he has not,
but rejoices for those which he has.
~ Epictetus

Psychological research finds that people's happiness levels are remarkably stable over the long-term. A possible explanation comes from studies in the psychology of gratitude. Yes, you read that correctly — being thankful just may be the secret to happiness.

The study* cited that people who were in the gratitude condition felt fully 25% happier — they were more optimistic about the future, they felt better about their lives.

The words "gratitude" and "grace" share a common Latin origin — *gratus*, meaning "pleasing" or "thankful." When you are in a deep state of gratitude, you may feel the presence of grace. Reflect on this. As we become more mindful of the present moment, we begin to recognize the things around us that we may have taken for granted. Recall for a moment how Anne LeClaire paused to watch two eider ducks dive in the water; how that moment gave her a connection and reverence for nature, for the beauty that surrounded her each day, and how she began to think about the many things for which she was grateful. (p. 48)

Gratitude unlocks the fullness of life.
It turns what we have into enough, and more.
It turns denial into acceptance, chaos to order, confusion to
clarity. It can turn a meal into a feast, a house into a home,
a stranger into a friend. Gratitude makes sense of our past,
brings peace for today, and creates a vision for tomorrow.
~ Melody Beattie

Learning to practice gratitude is one of life's most valuable lessons. As Aristotle taught us, all virtues have value and the virtue of gratitude helps to increase feelings of satisfaction with our lives and keeps us from falling into the excess of a greedy or entitled frame of mind.

There are many simple, yet powerful ways to practice gratitude on a daily basis.

- Thank, separately, both the cashier and the bagger at the grocery store.
- Send a hand-written thank you note when you receive a gift, however small.
- Make "thank you" a common phrase in your vocabulary.
- Keep a gratitude journal. Each night write 1-3 things for which you were grateful during the day. (Use the pages provided below to get you started.)

> *Gratitude is not only the greatest of virtues,*
> *but the parent of all the others.*
> ~ Cicero

*Emmons, R. A., & McCullough, M. E. (2003). Counting blessings versus burdens: An experimental investigation of gratitude and subjective well-being in daily life. *Journal of Personality and Social Psychology,* 84(2), 377-389

My Gratitude Journal

Date:_____   **Today, I am grateful for…**

_____

_____

_____

_____

Date:_____   **Today, I am grateful for…**

_____

_____

_____

_____

Date:_____   **Today, I am grateful for…**

_____

_____

_____

_____

Date:_____   **Today, I am grateful for...**

_____

_____

_____

_____

_____

Date:_____   **Today, I am grateful for...**

_____

_____

_____

_____

_____

Date:_____   **Today, I am grateful for...**

_____

_____

_____

_____

_____

Date:_____ **Today, I am grateful for…**

_____

_____

_____

_____

_____

Date:_____ **Today, I am grateful for…**

_____

_____

_____

_____

_____

Date:_____ **Today, I am grateful for…**

_____

_____

_____

_____

_____

Serenity…

The Serenity Prayer

*God grant me the serenity
to accept the things I cannot change;
the courage to change the things I can;
and the wisdom to know the difference.*

Written by theologian Reinhold Niebuhr, most people are familiar with this first stanza. However, Niebuhr's prayer also included these concepts:

- Living one day at a time
- Enjoying one moment at a time
- Accepting hardships as the pathway to peace

Often we become anxious about things we cannot change: the economy, the weather, our commute to work. Recognizing the difference between what we can and cannot change can help us live more peaceful and productive lives. Patience and perseverance leads to success in our endeavors.

The Serenity Prayer has special meaning to those who are often looking for peace during times of turmoil, despair, or uncertainty in their lives. Closely associated with Alcoholics Anonymous and other 12-step programs, the Serenity Prayer offers strength and calm into those seeking a more stable life.

> *Calmness of mind is one of the beautiful jewels of wisdom. It is the result of long and patient effort in self-control.*
> *~ James Allen*

More Wisdom Through The Ages

There is nothing permanent, except change.
~ Heraclitus

The unexamined life is not worth living.
~ Socrates

To know what to ask is already to know half.
~ Aristotle

Man is what he thinks about all day long.
~ Ralph Waldo Emerson

The greatest discovery of our generation is that human beings can alter their lives by altering their attitudes of mind. As you think, so shall you be.
~ William James

Nothing in life is to be feared, it is only to be understood.
~ Marie Curie

It is not the critic who counts; not the man who points out how the strong man stumbles...The credit belongs to the man who is actually in the arena...who strives valiantly; who errs...because there is no effort without error...Who knows in the end the triumph of high achievement, and...if he fails, at least fails while daring greatly.
~ Teddy Roosevelt, excerpt from speech "Citizenship in a Republic"

Live as if you were to die tomorrow. Learn as if you were to live forever.
~ Mahatma Gandhi

I do one thing that scares me every day.
~ Eleanor Roosevelt

Nothing in the world can take the place of persistence. Talent will not; nothing is more common than unsuccessful men with talent. Genius will not; unrewarded genius is almost a proverb. Education will not; the world is full of educated derelicts. Persistence and determination alone are omnipotent.
~ Calvin Coolidge

If you're going through hell, keep going.
~ Winston Churchill

If opportunity doesn't knock, build a door.
~ Milton Berle

If you don't fail regularly you are not trying hard enough things.
~ Ivan Sutherland

Nobody can go back and start a new beginning, but anyone can start today and make a new ending.
~ Maria Robinson

If you always do what you have always done, then you'll always have what you've already got.
~ Unknown

We lie the loudest when we lie to ourselves.
~ Eric Hoffer

The pessimist sees difficulty in every opportunity; the optimist sees opportunity in every difficulty.
~ Cory Everson

Watch your thoughts; they become words.
Watch your words; they become actions.
Watch your actions; they become habits.
Watch your habits; they become character.
Watch your character; it becomes your destiny.
- Frank Law

Our deepest fear is not that we are inadequate. Our deepest fear is that we are powerful beyond measure. It is our light, not our darkness, that frightens us.

We ask ourselves, who am I to be brilliant, gorgeous, talented, and fabulous? Actually, who are you not to be? You are a child of God. Your playing small doesn't serve the world.

There is nothing enlightened about shrinking so that other people wont feel insecure around us. We were born to make manifest the glory of God that is within us. It is not just in some of us; it is in everyone of us. And as we let our own light shine, we unconsciously give other people permission to do the same. As we are liberated from our own fear, our presence automatically liberates others.
~ Marianne Williamson, from *A Return to Love*

Tears are God's gift to us. Our holy water. They heal us as they flow.
~ Rita Schiano, from *Sweet Bitter Love*

Quotes That Inspire You

In the midst of winter,
I finally learned there was in me
an invincible summer.
~ Albert Camus

The above quote was featured on a card I received from one of my college philosophy professors. It arrived at a time in my life when my world seemed so cold and bleak. I was twenty-two years old, living in Ohio while attending graduate school. I was still reeling psychically from the murder of my father just days before Christmas that past December. It was my winter of discontent.

Yet, those fifteen words by Albert Camus sparked an inner strength, a flicker of joy, and awakened a dormant, indomitable soul. While many of you cannot identify with the murder of a loved one, I know everyone can identify an event in their life that has staggered them, made them feel helpless.

This final exercise is based on an assignment I gave my students in the Stress Management class. They were to each submit a quotation or passage that they found to be inspirational and motivating, and include a 1-2 page explanation as to why the saying had meaning to them, and how it affected their actions.

Okay, dear reader, time to do your homework….

A Quote That Inspired Me

Quote: _____

_____

_____

_____

Source: _____

What this quote means to me:_____

_____

_____

_____

_____

_____

_____

_____

_____

_____

_____

_____

_____

_____

_____

_____

_____

Live A Flourishing Life

How this quote has affected my life:_____

_____

_____

_____

_____

_____

_____

_____

_____

_____

_____

_____

_____

_____

_____

_____

_____

_____

_____

_____

Part Four:

Relax and Flourish

About Progressive Relaxation and Mindful Breathing

Relaxation techniques allow us to release tension
and focus the energy of our mind and body.
~ Dr. Mehmet Oz

I've included with this workbook a CD with two exercises. The first track, *Relax and Flourish*, guides you through a progressive relaxation technique. The thrust of this exercise is to help you learn how to:

- Recognize the difference between tense and relaxed muscles
- Visualize peace and ease flowing through your body
- Progressively relax all the muscles of your body, from the top of your head and down to your toes
- Focus on breathing and releasing tension with each breath

> *Practicing regular, mindful breathing can be*
> *calming and energizing, and can even help*
> *with stress-related health problems ranging from*
> *panic attacks to digestive disorders.*
> ~ Andrew Weil, M.D.

The second track, *Breathe and Flourish,* will help you learn the technique of mindful breathing. The aim of mindful breathing is to quiet and focus the mind. The practice works primarily by withdrawing our attention from distracting thoughts and redirecting our attention to the physical sensations of the breath.

Each exercise takes less than fifteen minutes. Try alternating between them each until you are ready to make both a daily practice. You may want to start your day with the mindful breathing exercise and end your day with the progressive relaxation technique. Whichever you choose to do, make it a regular practice. The pages that follow with help you track and review your progress.

Go forth, now, and flourish…

How You Responded — Day 1

Were you able to identify tension sources in your body?

Yes_____No_____Unsure_____

If so, in what area of your body was the tension located?

_____

_____

_____

_____

Were you able to visualize "peace and ease"?

Yes_____No_____Unsure_____

If so, how would you describe the sensation?

_____

_____

_____

_____

_____

_____

_____

Were you able to shut our your thoughts

Yes_____   No_____

If not, what were you thinking about?

_____

_____

_____

_____

_____

_____

On a scale of 1 – 10, how much of the time was your mind racing?

#_____

Pinpoint the moment you were able to relax and focus on your breathing. How would you describe the shift in your consciousness?

_____

_____

_____

_____

_____

_____

_____

How You Responded — Day 2

Were you able to identify tension sources in your body?

Yes_____No_____Unsure_____

If so, in what area of your body was the tension located?

_____

_____

_____

_____

Were you able to visualize "peace and ease"?

Yes_____No_____Unsure_____

If so, how would you describe the sensation?

_____

_____

_____

_____

_____

_____

_____

Were you able to shut our your thoughts

Yes_____   No_____

If not, what were you thinking about?

_____

_____

_____

_____

_____

_____

On a scale of 1 – 10, how much of the time was your mind racing?

#_____

Pinpoint the moment you were able to relax and focus on your breathing. How would you describe the shift in your consciousness?

_____

_____

_____

_____

_____

_____

_____

How You Responded — Day 3

Were you able to identify tension sources in your body?

Yes_____No_____Unsure_____

If so, in what area of your body was the tension located?

_____

_____

_____

_____

Were you able to visualize "peace and ease"?

Yes_____No_____Unsure_____

If so, how would you describe the sensation?

_____

_____

_____

_____

_____

_____

_____

_____

Were you able to shut our your thoughts

Yes_____   No_____

If not, what were you thinking about?

_____

_____

_____

_____

_____

_____

On a scale of 1 – 10, how much of the time was your mind racing?

#_____

Pinpoint the moment you were able to relax and focus on your breathing. How would you describe the shift in your consciousness?

_____

_____

_____

_____

_____

_____

_____

_____

How You Responded — Day 4

Were you able to identify tension sources in your body?

Yes_____No_____Unsure_____

If so, in what area of your body was the tension located?

_____

_____

_____

_____

Were you able to visualize "peace and ease"?

Yes_____No_____Unsure_____

If so, how would you describe the sensation?

_____

_____

_____

_____

_____

_____

_____

_____

Live A Flourishing Life

Were you able to shut our your thoughts

Yes_____   No_____

If not, what were you thinking about?

_____

_____

_____

_____

_____

_____

On a scale of 1 – 10, how much of the time was your mind racing?

#_____

Pinpoint the moment you were able to relax and focus on your breathing. How would you describe the shift in your consciousness?

_____

_____

_____

_____

_____

_____

_____

_____

How You Responded — Day 5

Were you able to identify tension sources in your body?

Yes_____No_____Unsure_____

If so, in what area of your body was the tension located?

_____

_____

_____

_____

Were you able to visualize "peace and ease"?

Yes_____No_____Unsure_____

If so, how would you describe the sensation?

_____

_____

_____

_____

_____

_____

_____

Were you able to shut our your thoughts

Yes_____   No_____

If not, what were you thinking about?

_____

_____

_____

_____

_____

_____

On a scale of 1 – 10, how much of the time was your mind racing?

#_____

Pinpoint the moment you were able to relax and focus on your breathing. How would you describe the shift in your consciousness?

_____

_____

_____

_____

_____

_____

_____

_____

How You Responded — Day 6

Were you able to identify tension sources in your body?

Yes_____No_____Unsure_____

If so, in what area of your body was the tension located?

_____

_____

_____

_____

Were you able to visualize "peace and ease"?

Yes_____No_____Unsure_____

If so, how would you describe the sensation?

_____

_____

_____

_____

_____

_____

_____

_____

Were you able to shut our your thoughts

Yes_____   No_____

If not, what were you thinking about?

_____

_____

_____

_____

_____

On a scale of 1 – 10, how much of the time was your mind racing?

#_____

Pinpoint the moment you were able to relax and focus on your breathing. How would you describe the shift in your consciousness?

_____

_____

_____

_____

_____

_____

_____

_____

How You Responded — Day 7

Were you able to identify tension sources in your body?

Yes_____No_____Unsure_____

If so, in what area of your body was the tension located?

_____

_____

_____

_____

Were you able to visualize "peace and ease"?

Yes_____No_____Unsure_____

If so, how would you describe the sensation?

_____

_____

_____

_____

_____

_____

_____

Were you able to shut our your thoughts

Yes_____   No_____

If not, what were you thinking about?

_____

_____

_____

_____

_____

_____

On a scale of 1 – 10, how much of the time was your mind racing?

#_____

Pinpoint the moment you were able to relax and focus on your breathing. How would you describe the shift in your consciousness?

_____

_____

_____

_____

_____

_____

_____

_____

Bibliography

Barlow, David H. *Anxiety and Its Disorders: The Nature and Treatment of Anxiety and Panic.* New York: Guilford Press, 2002.

Breazeale, Dr. Ron. *Duct Tape Isn't Enough: Survival Skills for the 21ˢᵗ Century.* Portland, Maine: Bounce Back USA, 2009.

Butler, Pamela E. *Self-Assertion for Women.* New York: HarperCollins, 1992.

Cornell, Ann Weiser. *The Power of Focusing: A Practical Guide to Emotional Self-Healing.* Oakland, CA: New Harbinger Publications, 1996.

Coué, Emil. *Self-Mastery Through Conscious Autosuggestion.* Montana: Kessinger Publishing, 1922.

Cousins, Norman. *Anatomy of an Illness.* New York: W. W. Norton Company, 2005.

Covey, Stephen. R. *The 7 Habits of Highly Effective People.* New York: Simon & Schuster, 2004.

Davis, M., Robbins, E. Eshelman, M. Fanning, P. *The Relaxation & Stress Reduction Workbook.* Oakland, CA. New Harbinger Publications, 2008.

Dolan, S. L. *Stress, Self-Esteem, Health and Work.* New York: Palgrave Macmillan, 2006.

Frankl, Victor E. *Man's Search for Meaning.* Boston: Beacon Press 1959, 2006.

Goleman, D. *Emotional Intelligence.* New York: Bantam Books, 1995.

Helmstetter, Shad. *What to Say When You Talk to Your Self.* New York: Pocket Books, 1982.

Hiatt, Ph.D., Marta. *Mind Magic Techniques for Transforming Your Life.* Minnesota: Llewellyn Publications, 2005.

Jeffers, Susan. *Feel the Fear and Do It Anyway.* New York: Fawcett Columbine, 1987.

Kabat-Zinn, Jon. *Full Catastrophe Living: Using the Wisdom of Your Body and Mind to Face Stress and Illness.* New York: Delacorte, 1990.

165

Klein, Allen. *The Healing Power of Humor*. Los Angeles: Tarcher. 1989.

MacKanzie, Richard. *Self-Change Hypnosis,* Victoria. BC, Canada: Trafford Publishing, 2005.

McCurdy, Dennis. *Find A Way: A Guide to Getting the Most Out of Life.* Sturbridge, Massachusetts: Adam Beck Publishers, 2008.

McKay, Matthew, M. David, and P. Fanning. *Thoughts and Feelings: Taking Control of Your Moods and Your Life*, 3rd ed. Oakland, CA: New Harbinger Publications, 2007.

Murphy Ph.D, DD, Joseph. Revised by Ian McMahan, PH.D. *The Power of Your Subconscious Mind.* New York: Reward Books, 2000 (revised).

Pausch, Randy & Jeffrey Zaslow. *The Last Lecture.* New York: Hyperion, 2008.

Pelzer, David J. *Moving Forward: Taking the Lead in Your Life.* New York: Center Street, 2008.

Santangelo, Jodi. *Dynamic Affirmations.* New York: Morgan James Publishing, 2010.

Schiano, Rita. *Painting the Invisible Man.* Wilbraham, Massachusetts: The Reed Edwards Company, 2007.

Schiano, Rita. *Sweet BitterLove.* New York: Rising Tide Press, 1997.

Schuller, Robert H. *Tough Times Never Last, But Tough People Do!* Nashville: Bantam Book, 1984.

Seligman, Martin E.P. *Learned Optimism: How to Change Your Mind and Your Life.* New York: Vintage, 2006.

Siegel, Bernie. *Love, Medicine and Miracles.* New York: Harper & Row, 1990.

Smith, Manuel J. *When I Say No, I Feel Guilty.* New York: Bantam Books, 1985.

Strank, Jeremy. *Stress at Work: Management and Prevention.* Oxford: Elsevier Butterwork-Heinemann Publications, 2005.

Williamson, Marianne. *A Return to Love, Reflections on the Principles of A Course in Miracles.* New York: Harper-Perennial, 1992.

About The Author

Rita Schiano is an adjunct professor teaching both Philosophy and Stress Management courses. In addition, she is a stress management and resilience-building trainer. For more information on *Live A Flourishing Life* workshops and personal coaching sessions, visit Rita's web site, www.ritaschiano.com.

Rita is also a keynote speaker and author. Her novels, *Sweet Bitter Love* and *Painting the Invisible Man*, are available at www.reededwards.com.

NOTE: *Painting the Invisible Man* has been acknowledged as a story of courage and resilience. Based on true events in Rita Schiano's life, the book became a foundation of her personal resilience-building plan.

The story behind the story...

In 2001, while researching the online archives of her hometown newspaper for a client, freelance writer Rita Schiano stumbled upon archived stories about her father's murder and the possible mob connections that led to his death. This brief visit to her past inspired her to look deeply into the heart of her childhood. The journey she embarked on was nothing she could have ever anticipated. Rather than place her work into the harsh scrutiny of memoirs, Schiano developed her story through the eyes of a fictional character, Anna Matteo. It is the story of a stolen childhood, a family torn apart by the violence of mafia ties, and one young girl's resilient spirit that allowed her to rise above the hardships and seek solace in the most unusual ways.

Employing philosophical insight and a sardonic wit, Schiano vividly takes the reader through myriad brush strokes as her character paints the unfinished portraits of both her father and herself.

*For more reviews and information about *Painting the Invisible Man,* and to order signed, personalized copies, visit www.paintingtheinvisibleman.com